Owen McCafferty was born in Belfast in 1961. Educated at St. Augustine's Secondary School in the city and at the University of Ulster, he has had many plays produced for the stage. His latest play, *Shoot the Crow*, was nominated for the Best New Play category in 1997 *Irish Times/ESB* Irish Theatre Awards.

GW00468972

PLAYS & MONOLOGUES

PLAYS & MONOLOGUES

Shoot the Crow • Damage Done • The Waiting List
Freefalling • I Won't Dance Don't Ask Me • The Private Picture Show

OWEN McCAFFERTY

foreword by
Louis Muinzer

LAGAN PRESS
BELFAST
1998

Published by
Lagan Press
7 Lower Crescent, Belfast, BT7 1NR

ISBN: 1 873687 76 1
Author: McCafferty, Owen
Title: Plays & Monologues
1998

Cover: David Ganley and Anthony Brophy
in *Shoot the Crow* and Anne Bird and Miceal Murphy in *Freefalling*
(photographs courtesy of Druid Theatre Company, Galway
and Kabosh Theatre Company, Belfast)
Cover Design: December Publications
Set in New Baskerville
Printed by Noel Murphy Printing, Belfast

for my father, Gerry,
1934-1985

CONTENTS

Foreword

A Voice on Stage: The Plays of Owen McCafferty

In the six years since 1992, Owen McCafferty has established himself as one of Ireland's important new dramatists. In that time, his work has been staged by two of this island's major theatres, the Lyric in his native Belfast and the Druid in Galway, and brought to the Edinburgh Festival by the new and ambitious Kabosh company, whose McCafferty production won a major Fringe award. Clearly, the time is right for his groundbreaking plays to be gathered for publication, where both readers and prospective producers can take a long, close look at them.

McCafferty was born in Belfast in 1961; he was educated at St. Augustine's Secondary School and at the University of Ulster. His plays speak with the voice of his home town: a voice that is earthy, streetwise and profane, sprinkled when appropriate with expletives, rhymed slang and less-than-middle-class idiom. And yet the language of his plays is no mere transcript of 'uncultivated' Belfast chat. On the contrary, it embodies a creative—and I believe successful—attempt to forge a strong dramatic language from the speech of the Belfast streets. In this attempt, he has had notable predecessors like Sam Thompson and John Boyd and later practitioners like Graham Reid and Martin Lynch—writers who have all helped condition the language of our stage. I myself am only an inside outsider, a foreign listener among Belfast voices, and it may be that even my long residence here has left me less expert than the 'local punters' themselves. For what it is worth, though, neither my memory nor my ear recalls a single Belfast dramatist who can match Owen McCafferty's gift of speech. When he wants to, he can lift the dialect to the level of fierce and joyful poetry, can intensify its rhythm and fling out its imagery and idiom with that joy-in-language that is the hallmark of the finest Irish dramatists. Almost a century ago, J.M. Synge shaped a fabulous stage speech from the lonely coastal voices of western Ireland. A few decades later, Sean O'Casey shaped another from the eastern, urban voices of the Dublin he both knew and heard. Owen McCafferty's language represents the same verbal tradition as it turns north and heads smack into the our own uproarious, tragic, unquenchable city on the Lagan. And that turn is the right one for our theatre: Synge's voices inspire nostalgia, the rural and the timeless, but they have given way to city voices that speak dramatically of modern Ireland: first in O'Casey's city of the Easter Rising and now in McCafferty's city of the Troubles.

In speaking of McCafferty as a dramatist of Troubled Belfast, I am aware of a considerable irony, for the politically-motivated traumas of the last quarter century are by no means central to his work, as they are to that of many northern dramatists. Of the plays printed here, only *The Waiting List* (1994), a dramatic monologue, is staged against a backdrop of suspicion, bigotry and violence. If we want plays about the Troubles, we must look elsewhere—and, to be honest, many of us who have lived with the reality for a quarter of a century are glad to give them a rest. The lasting creative value of this terrible period lies in its spirit, not in its subject matter, for it has awakened us all to the resilience and deep-rooted humanity of Belfast people. In the old days, our city was good for a kitchen comedy or a bit of crack: the Troubles have "changed, changed utterly" that stereotype into flesh and blood. Broad Belfast has become Deep Belfast, and both its people and its language have taken on a new dimension. And lest I be misunderstood, let me add at once that Deep Belfast is far funnier and more gutsy than the old Broad variety: because we have come to feel with and respect the people, their free-wheeling and outrageous language can share their newly-appreciated depth on our stage— can laugh or cry, can plow through society or spotlight the heart.

McCafferty's staging of this enriched language reveals clearly its immense theatrical possibilities, its emotional range. In *Freefalling* (1996), it becomes the vehicle of bitterness, irony and dream, of violence and implicit tragedy. In *I Won't Dance Don't Ask Me* (1993), the collection's other one-hander or monologue, it blends wisecrack, and reverie. In *Shoot the Crow* (1997), an aromatic voice-quartet for a team of tilers, it dances with a joy that it has seldom known on this side of *The Playboy of the Western World.* There, and indeed elsewhere in McCafferty's plays, the idiom may shock those attuned to the verbal niceties of Wilde and other classic comedians, but no Belfast school child or casual pedestrian will find it at all rarified. In using it, McCafferty is not trying to murder 'polite' expression, but simply to open our theatre to the full range of living speech. In any case, the verbal delights of *Shoot the Crow* depend upon its wild-roving poetry, not its profanity. It reflects McCafferty's ability to use street speech for the ends of rhythmic, flexible and unhackneyed expression. Clearly, it is a gift that he is developing as his experience grows.

Having focused so far on the Irish/Belfast side of McCafferty's plays, however, I am in danger of misrepresenting them both for the local and foreign reader of this collection: these plays are not tied to locale and dialect, but simply grounded in them. By intent and performance alike, McCafferty explores themes of placeless human significance: themes that involve the individual's unfulfillable dreams, his imprisonment in his social world, his need to work, his ties to a parent or a child, his encrusted, perhaps inarticulate tenderness— even his underlying decency, if such a word can still be used in these disenchanted times. These and other themes roll through the following plays like skilfully varied melodies—human melodies, not local street-songs.

Karl Wallace, director of the Kabosh *Freefalling* production, brilliantly demonstrated how readily McCafferty's 'hometown' drama can be related to the broader vistas of our times, when he responded to the cinema references in the script and placed the play's tragedy-bound young Belfast couple in the context of the Hollywood *film noir*, using a loop of American film clips to underline their story. The result was both movie-like and moving. As the production revealed, McCafferty's script deals with human themes that are relevant wherever young people leap over the precipice of a constricting life to gain a moment of doomed freedom:

We jump—a moment, the only moment—alive—free—
floating—we smile and kiss. *Eddie, Eddie, Eddie.* Bang, splat,
dead.

Belfast? OK—but also Paris, Chicago and Rio—and probably
Beijing.

The Private Picture Show (1994) also explores drop outs, but ones
whose free-fall is metaphorical and ambiguous. They are the
appealing, vulnerable human presences in a young writer's search
for something troublesome called 'truth'. Like *The Waiting List*, the
story of a done-by life in a do-in time, this play strikes me as a very
personal piece of writing, but one in which the playwright is more
complexly present than in the monologue. In *The Private Picture
Show*, I suspect that McCafferty is both Iggy, the questing author who
lives in the midst of the off-beat lodgers, and Linda, the photojournalist
who has left them to live outside, but who returns to record them all
with her camera. But if this play is indeed personal, its title rather
belies its character, for *The Private Picture Show* is certainly not private
in any restrictive sense. It belongs with Joyce's *A Portrait of the Artist
as a Young Man* and every other piece of writing in which an author
explores himself as both insider and outsider, as both participant
and observer. Ultimately, it is a play about all of us who engage in our
own wondering dialogue with experience—who stand on the lighted
stage, yet sit in the dark auditorium looking on.

The same breadth of humanity also bedrocks the seemingly
small, inconsequential world of the four tilers in *Shoot the Crow*. They
are local workmen on the make and going nowhere, but cemented
together by a depth of feeling not often reflected in their speech.
They are Belfast through and through. Walk through any
neighbourhood in McCafferty's city and when you spot a clutch of
craftsmen yarning and humping their way through some house
renovations, them's the very boys. Nevertheless, if you stage this play
in Burkino Faso with African workmen speaking French or in
Alabama with four poor whites drawling away in Dixie, you will find
your work easier than you think: that is because Petesy, Randolph,

Socrates and Ding-Ding will remain essentially—and triumphantly—the same. You may have to revamp their lingo, but you won't have to translate their bottom-of-the-ladder character and spirit. It hit town long ago.

And are Petesy, Randolph, Socrates and Ding-Ding really so 'working class' at heart? Might we not meet comparably hopeful but hard-pressed chancers in the management suite of a major conglomerate in Houston or Tokyo? Let's hope so, for it would be a dark day indeed if such rich and meaningful humanity as theirs were the exclusive property of the poor.

Of Gus McMahon in *I Won't Dance Don't Ask Me*, however, I need have no doubts: he is alive and feeling useless and jawing with his cat in Houston, Tokyo and dozens of other cities besides Belfast. He belongs to a score of social circles, speaks a hundred languages and has a thousand legitimate beefs. He a member of that flourishing sub-species of *homo erectus*, Redundant Man: man on the shelf, deprived of his dignity, tormented by a past that his empty present cannot block out. One of my favourite McCaffertys, this one-man-show is the very model of what a 'local' play should be: rooted in its own soil but spreading its branches over the landscape of Everyman.

The far-ranging relevance of McCafferty's themes and characters is matched by his breadth of form: there may be an element of realism in his stagecraft, as there is in his language, but he is no conventional realist. It is revealing that, along with other favourite dramatists like David Mamet, Tom Murphy and Sam Shepherd, he lists the great Franco-Rumanian absurdist Eugene Ionesco. In the present collection, McCafferty's freedom of form is found everywhere. In *Freefalling*, the two main characters play various additional roles and set the scene with speech, movement, two straight chairs and two tables. In *The Private Picture Show,* Iggy's room contains some furniture, but is simply "defined by a square of light centre stage"; the 'off-stage' characters sit in chairs by its side. In *I Won't Dance Don't Ask Me*, the interior is also defined by a square of light; it contains only "an armchair draped with two or three sheets of wall paper" and an optional bottle of Guinness. In *The Waiting List*, the actor works on a stage that is completely empty "except for the frame of a pram which the actor can use as he pleases." In spirit, at least, *Shoot the Crow* is the most realistic of the plays, for the workaday world of its tilers is a functional part of the story. Even here, however, the setting need be only semi-naturalistic. If I were staging it, I would make use of very simple, evocative decor and let the pungent dialogue do the rest.

With regard to style, however, the shortest and perhaps slightest piece in the collection, *Damage Done* (1994), is probably the most promising of all. In this brief two-hander, an elderly—indeed 'ancient'—couple seated in armchairs speak the language of the five other plays, but seem to evoke the stage-land of Beckett and Ionesco. If Owen McCafferty develops his style in this direction, he will soon be scripting plays with a new and highly unusual Belfast aura. Next time and one way or another, we may even bump into Godot on the Ormeau bus.

On the whole, then, this drama collection represents both an achievement and a promise: the achievement is there in the six plays which follow and the promise is that of new and forward-looking plays that are sure to follow them. Owen McCafferty has a flair for the living language and the ability to make it speak of and for a humanity that wanders far beyond his native streets; he has also a theatrical eye that sees beyond the limiting precincts of realism into the landscape of imaginative stagecraft. But having made those confident assertions, I had better just shoot the crow [1] and let McCafferty's readers judge for themselves. I don't think they will be disappointed.

Louis Muinzer
Belfast, December, 1997

[1] In certain Belfast circles, people would have written *go* in this sentence. However, both these repressed linguists and initially-unnerved foreign readers will enjoy translating the rhymed jargon that figures so prominently in McCafferyese.

SHOOT THE CROW
(1997)

Shoot the Crow was first performed in the Druid Theatre, Druid Lane, Galway on 26th February 1997. It was directed by David Parnell. The cast was as follows:

Petesy, *36 years-old*	Anthony Brophy
Socrates, *39 years-old*	David Ganley
Randolph, *19 years-old*	Fergal McElherron
Ding-Ding, *65 years-old*	Patrick Waldron
Designer	Paul McCauley
Lighting Designer	Tina MacHugh
Production Manager	Maurice Power
Stage Director	Mairead McGrath
Technical Stage Manager	Bernie Walsh
Assistant Stage Manager	Rosie O'Connell
Technicians/Operators	Pete Ashton, Clair Burkitt
Set Construction	Alan Clarke, Frank Gleeson, Eoin O'Flaherty
Scenic Artist	Ger Sweeney
Wardrobe	Gabrielle McGrath
Fight Director	Rod Goodall
Dialogue Coach	Andrea Ainsworth

The play takes place during the working day of four tilers on a building site. They are tiling adjoining rooms—a public toilet and a shower area. The stage is divided in two. There is a door leading to 'on site' ie, off-stage and another between the two rooms. It is Friday, the end of the working week.

DING-DING *asleep.* RANDOLPH *enters from 'on site' carrying two cups of tea and a magazine.*

RANDOLPH: Petesy an' Socrates are stayin' down in the other room—talkin' a lotta shite—here's your tea—don't mind me now just you have a wee kip there an' I'll run about like a blue-arsed fly gettin' you fuckin' tea—tea in the special cup. [*Sets the cup down and circles it.*] Don't touch the cup—Ding-Ding's special cup—the cup—fuck you an' yer cup—who needs cups when ye have bikin' magazines, that's what I say. [*He sits and opens his magazine.*] *Vroom,* fuckin' *vroom.* [DING-DING *wakes.*] Look at that, a large set a wheels with some wee doll wrapped roun' ye, is that the business or what—I get the readies together that's me, on the bike an' offski. Long y'reckon it take to do that, save for a bike—did I tell ye that's what I'm doin', savin' for a bike? Long? Couldn't take that long like, a few squid every week, a few squid, join a club an' that—have'm, like Christmas clubs only for motor bikes. Long d'ye reckon? Need a licence first like—that'll not be a problem me an' ma mate been practisin' on push bikes, same type a crack like innit, not as heavy or as fast but it's the same neck a the woods like. Cuppla a shillins every week, licence, bike an' then it's the get yer Philias Fogg gear on ye' an' away we go except I'd have some wee doll with me instead a that dopey French geezer he has

21

knockin' about with him plus I'd be on a bike all the time instead a that trains, steamers an' balloon chats. Wanna see the ones in the magazine I have, magic. Wanna see the wee dolls innit, fuckin' unbelievable. Big three wheel efforts—just lie back an' sally on. Big money they are like, big readies, take more than a few quid there every week. A wee one do me, so long as y'can fit two on it. Go through that tunnel dixie, a cuppla hours it's all pernod and distilled water an' bung us another clatter a them frogs legs. A wee doll on the back a the bike wingin' yer way through France an' yous boys fucked, slappin' shit coloured tiles on some oul doll's wall. D'ya reckon that Ding-Ding—what d'ya reckon?

DING-DING: Y'know fuck all, y'know that, fuck all about fuck all.

RANDOLPH: I'll be whistlin' dixie with the camels round the Kasbah— no sweat about it—*vroom, vroom.*

DING-DING: Aye, vroom, vroom.

RANDOLPH: What—I've just told ye what I'm gonna do regardin' me an' the world an' the big picture—what's the problem here—ye have t'make plans don't ye, isn't that what we're all about makin' plans an' that, gettin' the stuff ahead a ye sorted out.

DING-DING: Make plans—what for?

RANDOLPH: What for—what does that mean, what for? The future— that's the crack, ye do shit now so ye can sort yerself out for the future—there's no point in graftin' an' that if it's not gonna help ye paddle yer own dixie later in life is there?

DING-DING: That right—what's that?

RANDOLPH: What d'ye mean, what is it? It's a letter, a letter.

DING-DING: Correct. A letter—who's it from?

RANDOLPH: C'mon til.

DING-DING: Heavy Hole—it's a letter from Heavy Hole—fucker.

RANDOLPH: Didn't send me one.

DING-DING: No, he didn't send you one. It's a thank you letter, not typed now, handwritten, the personal touch. He's thankin' me for my time—doesn't say that but that's what it means—the

time I spent helpin' him t'get wherever he's goin'. Fuck'im. A
lifetime spent graftin' an' ye end up with a thank you note—
handwritten, we mustn't forget that. Today's the day, Randolph
kid—today's the day.

RANDOLPH: Thought ye weren't retirin' til next week.

DING-DING: No—t'day.

RANDOLPH: Did he drop ye anythin', sort ye out for a few extra
squid.

DING-DING: Ye only get what's comin' t'ye in this world son—in my
case that adds up to fuck all squared.

RANDOLPH: Fuck'im.

DING-DING: Correct, fuck'im.

RANDOLPH: No more graftin' for ye, yer home on a boat that way—
feet up in front a the dixie, few bets, eye the gee gees, cuppla
swallys in the afternoon, fuckin' landed ye are.

DING-DING: That's what a mean, Randolph son, that's what I'm
tellin' ye, ye know fuck all about fuck all—see that letter, that's
what all yer plans amount til, fuck all.

RANDOLPH: A few quid away a week—I know what am at—I'll not
be hangin' aroun' for any fuckin' letter from some geezer who
wouldn't recognise yer coupin if he passed ye in the street—
fuck 'at.

DING-DING: Go now, do it now, see if ye don't yer goose an' ducked.
Longer ye spend doin' this tighter the noose gets round yer
fuckin' neck an' after a while it's you that tightens it 'cause ye
get used to the feel a the rope. Do it now, get the bike now an'
go now.

RANDOLPH: What with, I need t'earn some readies t'get it don't a?

DING-DING: Fuckin' steal it if ye have to, do whatever ye have t'do—
all I'm sayin' is don't let fuck all pass ye by—thinkin' about
somethin' unless ye do it does nothin' but fuck ye up.

RANDOLPH: I work, I earn readies, I get the bike—that's it, there's
nothin' else to it—simple.

DING-DING: Work—work—y'know what work is, it's a fuckin' con—
work lets ye think ye can sprint like a gazelle, then it straps

fuckin' lead boots roun' yer plates a meat. I've a few shillins in ma sky rocket look at me I'm a king—only problem is, son, the few shillins is never enough to buy yerself a fuckin' crown—ye always think the crown's on the cards though, it must be other people wear them, until one day yer standin' in some shit-hole talkin' t'some kid with a handwritten letter in yer pocket sayin' thank you for yer trouble—it's a fuckin' con. An' know what the real beauty about all that is, the real sting in the tail? Ye can't do without it, 'cause if ye don't have it yer napper goes—no work an' the heads away.

RANDOLPH: Stop givin' me grief Ding-Ding will ye?

DING-DING: I'm tryin' to help ye here. What is it the bike means t'ye, escape, freedom, gettin' t'fuck out, doin' yer own thing, bein' yer own man, that what it means? I'll help ye get it.

RANDOLPH: You a big sackful a readies planked somewhere, aye?

DING-DING: There's a pallet a tiles lyin' roun' the front there, right?

RANDOLPH: Aye.

DING-DING: We'll steal them.

RANDOLPH: Getta fuck—what an' get nathered like that plumber fella the other day.

DING-DING: Fuck him.

RANDOLPH: Nothin' t'do with him, it's t'do with gettin' caught.

DING-DING: Ye want the bike don't ye, this is a way a gettin' it, the only way a gettin' it. I'll help ye out.

RANDOLPH: How ye helpin' me out? I didn't suggest it—helpin' yerself out—gettin back at Heavy Hole or somethin'?

DING-DING: Fuck all t'do with Heavy Hole.

RANDOLPH: What?

DING-DING: What what?

RANDOLPH: What's innit for you besides that deep inner feelin' of warmth ye get from helpin' a workmate—that you didn't much give a fuck about before?

DING-DING: D'ye want it or don't ye?

RANDOLPH: What do you want?

DING-DING: Same as you.

RANDOLPH: What's that?

DING-DING: Not to be trapped—not to wake up in the mornin' an' wish ye had some other punter's life 'cause yer's isn't the shit you thought it was cracked up to be.

RANDOLPH: After t'day ye can do that can't ye, no pressure on ye, do whatever ye want, ye've time t'do that now, isn't that what it's all about, retirin' an' that, time t'ease off or whatever.

DING-DING: I don't want time, that's the fuckin' point, time's no good to ye when ye've been used t'not havin' any—it fucks ye up—I don't want that.

RANDOLPH: What then what?

DING-DING: A winda cleaner—I'm gonna be a winda cleaner.

RANDOLPH: Getta fuck—winda cleaner—aye, winda cleaner, I know, aye.

DING-DING: Somethin' wrong with that—it's not gonna make me Rockafella but it'll get me a few shillins every week an' give me somethin' t'do—that's all I'm lookin, a few shillins an' somethin' t'do.

RANDOLPH: Yer gonna steal like so ye can be a winda cleaner?

DING-DING: Correct.

RANDOLPH: This might seem like an obvious question to you Ding-Ding, 'cause at the moment ye seem t'be workin' on a different type of a fuckin' level from the rest of us, but why do ye need a chunk a readies in order t'become a fuckin' winda cleaner— ye gonna buy a gold plated bucket aye?

DING-DING: I have t'buy somebody else's roun' off them that's why. I was panickin' about this retirement chat then somethin' happened an' I thought that'll do me. There's this oul lad lives two doors down from me—oul lad? That's fuckin' good, fella's only two years older than me. He's a winda cleaner, couppla week's back he couped off the ladder an' fucked his leg up— can't clean windas no more. I met him—limpin' his way round for a few pints, sittin' with other fuckers like himself all hatin' each other for bein' there. I'm talkin' to him, he's tellin' me about his leg an' that—I kept thinkin' t'myself he's fucked, ye

could see it in his lamps, dead, empty, no fuckin' spark in them
y'know—nothin' t'fill his time with ye see, his napper's gone,
he's fucked. That can't happen to me Randolph son—they'll
find that oul lad in six months time sittin' in his chair, stiff as
a board, cold as ice, dead for four days an' no fucker know
about it—that's not on Randolph kid. That's no way for any
human t'be. He's sellin' his roun'—first come first served—if
I get in there now I'm in business.

RANDOLPH: I don't get that, that doesn't make any sense t'me—
somethin' ye like doin' aye, I can understan' that, but where's
the pleasure in standin' half-way up a ladder, wet, monkeys,
wipin' the suds of some fucker's window—I don't get that, the
thinkin' behind that's all up the left.

DING-DING: Fuck all that, what I'm doin has got fuck all t'do with
you right—this is about you, you want readies towards yer
bikin' fund, well this is an opportunity—that's all ye gotta
concern yerself with fuck all else.

RANDOLPH: What about Petesy and Socrates, say anythin' t'them,
what about them?

DING-DING: Just me an' you, nothin' t'do with them, it's just me an'
you.

RANDOLPH: Say fuck all?

DING-DING: Say fuck all—between me an' you nobody else's business.

RANDOLPH: They were involved ye'd have t'split it four ways then
wouldn't ye?

DING-DING: Ye would.

RANDOLPH: Fuck that.

DING-DING: Half better than a quarter.

RANDOLPH: You got all the gear then?

DING-DING: What gear?

RANDOLPH: The black gear, you got all the black gear.

DING-DING: Black gear?

RANDOLPH: Tights, jumpers, gloves, those woolly chats ye pull over
yer napper.

DING-DING: Ropes and pulleys.

RANDOLPH: Aye.

DING-DING: Helicopter be handy.

RANDOLPH: Helicopter?

DING-DING: We're shiftin' tiles into a van at lunchtime, we're not stormin' the fuckin' embassy.

RANDOLPH: Lunchtime—lunchtime? That's fuckin' daylight that is.

DING-DING: Correct—we'll not need fuckin' torches then either will wa? Place is empty at lunchtime no hassle. Fire the tiles into the van, shift them, plank them, back later.

RANDOLPH: That all like, nothin' else no?

DING-DING: What?

RANDOLPH: I don't know just seems very normal like very ordinary or somethin'.

DING-DING: We're just stealin' tiles Randolph son, if tilers are gonna steal somethin' tiles seems like the obvious thing y'know. If we worked down a diamond mine now that be a different matter but things bein' what they are we're stuck with the fuckin' tiles.

RANDOLPH: Talk me through it again.

DING-DING: I just fuckin' said.

RANDOLPH: Talk me through it.

DING-DING: Lunch—tiles—van—shift—plank—sell—bingo.

RANDOLPH: Not need masks then.

DING-DING: Don't fuck me about boy.

RANDOLPH: I wanna wear a mask, I want it t'be at night, cut the fence gear with them big clanky scissors, drug the guard dogs with meat an' pills an' shit—a robbery y'know, like a real robbery— pity I didn't have the bike, quick get away—offski.

[DING-DING *grabs* RANDOLPH *by the throat.*]

DING-DING: This isn't a joke. I can't have ye fuckin' things up for me y'understand—ye can't fuck things up.

RANDOLPH: Yer hurtin' me.

DING-DING: Either yer doin it or yer not, but don't think ye can fuckin' mess me about on this.

RANDOLPH: I'm not.

[DING-DING *lets go*.]

DING-DING: If ye want somethin' badly enough ye take risks to get it—do y'want it or don't ye?

RANDOLPH: I don't know—what do you think—I don't know.

DING-DING: I'm not tellin' ye what t'do, you make yer own decisions—know yer own mind an' do what ye think's best.

RANDOLPH: If we're caught I'm fucked.

DING-DING: An' if we're not?

RANDOLPH: If we're not, I'm half-way there.

DING-DING: *Vroom, vroom* Randolph, *vroom vroom.*

RANDOLPH: Lunchtime?

DING-DING: Lunchtime.

[SOCRATES *and* PETESY *enter other room from 'on site'.*]

PETESY: If it's not in the other room it has t'be here or there.

SOCRATES: Aye, whatever. Do ye understan' what I'm sayin' about this—it's like ye were on a journey an' yer lookin' at the scenery an' shit as ye go along then ye arrive where yer meant t'be at, but if somebody was to say t'ye what road did ye take, how'd ye get here, ye wouldn't be able t'fuckin' say—that's the type a thing I'm talkin' about—understan' what I'm sayin'?

PETESY: You have a look for it, I'll check on these two.

SOCRATES: Yer not listenin' to me.

PETESY: Just have a jeff juke about the place will ye?

SOCRATES: Aye.

PETESY [*enters other room*]: He's doin' my fuckin' napper in again.

DING-DING: His head's gone.

PETESY: We're on journeys now that have no roads or somethin'—doin' my fuckin' napper in—come in t'do a day's graft ye end up slappin' on tiles with one a them fuckin' Tibetan chats that sit on their jam roll an' do their nappers in with thinkin'.

DING-DING: His head's gone.

PETESY: Aye.

DING-DING: Aye.

PETESY: What's the crack in here, ye's weltin' away at this or what?

DING-DING: Finished up there, aye?

PETESY: Bitta groutin' just—have to be red up today now.

DING-DING: Aye.

PETESY: Ye gettin' plenty a work outta him Ding-Ding, aye?

RANDOLPH: I'm alright.

PETESY: Just you keep cleanin' the buckets—never enough clean buckets, always need clean buckets Ding-Ding don't ye?

DING-DING: Oh aye—clean buckets.

PETESY: Got one dipped in bronze, do ye for yer retirement chat.

DING-DING: Aye.

PETESY: No more graftin'—pig in shit, wha?

DING-DING: Aye.

PETESY: Aye. Yous two see a delivery note lyin' about, no?

DING-DING: What ye want it for?

PETESY: Check the adhesive on the job.

DING-DING: Nah.

PETESY: If he's nothin' t'do Ding-Ding fire him in with us.

DING-DING: Aye.

RANDOLPH: Plenty t'do.

PETESY: Day's work kill ye.

RANDOLPH: Aye, I know.

PETESY: Away back in here with the Oracle.

DING-DING: His head's away.

[PETESY *exits next door.* RANDOLPH *makes masturbatory gesture after him.*]

PETESY: Two tossers. Ye find that?

SOCRATES: Wha?

PETESY: What'ye mean what, I said to ye have a butcher's for the delivery note.

SOCRATES: Fuck the delivery note.

PETESY: It's important. I wanna see if these tiles are on it or not.

SOCRATES: Fuck the tiles.

PETESY: Fuck the delivery note—fuck the tiles—we'll all just sit here with our heads jammed up our onion will wa?

SOCRATES: Delivery note—that it like, that where we are—aye?

PETESY: Yes.

SOCRATES: I'm tryin' to make sense of somethin' here, understan' what I'm sayin'? I'm tryin' t'throw a curve ball, have a look at things from a different dixie, a different perspective, know what a mean?

PETESY [*looking for delivery note*]: No.

SOCRATES: Tilt the beam of light that's fuckin' dixin' down on us at a different angle y'know.

PETESY: Aye.

SOCRATES: I'm standin' at a bus stop other mornin'. Monday mornin' early—this guy I know from when I was a kid stanin' across the way—there's two winos waitin' t'get their starter for the day, he queues up with them. I'm thinkin' he's goin' in for a packet a smokes on his way t'work—he's a plumber or somethin' fucked like that—the place opens an' the three a them are like greyhounds outta the trap—he didn't get smokes, he bought a carry out, couldn't even be bothered fuckin' puttin' it in a bag, four tins a that rocket fuel gear in his hand—doesn't give a fuck who sees him 'cause his head's fixed on the gargle—I used t'kick football with this guy now he's millin' four tins a piss yer begs gear t'wake him up, t'get him sorted out—it frightened me y'know—lookin' at him fucked me up.

PETESY: Some fella ye played headers with turned into a wino—what?

SOCRATES: What happened t'that guy, how'd he arrive where he's at, what happened between bein' a kid an' doin' all that shit and millin' tins up an entry on a fuckin' Monday mornin'? What happened?

PETESY: Ye gonna help me look for this?

SOCRATES: Know what a realised when a was lookin' at this guy, he had his own life—that meant I was living out my life but I'd never fuckin' noticed that before, know what I'm sayin', I wasn't aware of my own life.

PETESY: Look under the tool box.

SOCRATES: Fuck the delivery note. I'm not interested.

PETESY: Look under the tool box.

SOCRATES: Fuck the delivery note, fuck the box. If yer not aware of yer own life it means that ye haven't really participated in the shit that happens t'ye so ye end up at a certain point thinkin' how the fuck did I get here, like there was no control over it y'know. I'm doin' this, I'm doin that—I'm separated, I haven't seen her and the wee lad for a cuppla months—what's all that about, how'd that happen—was it always gonna happen, could I have stopped it from happenin'—what does shit like that mean?

PETESY: I can't find it—no delivery note—the tiles don't exist— happy days.

SOCRATES: What d'ye reckon—it's like do we live our own lives or do we live them through other people or what—what d'ye think?

PETESY: Don't know. They don't exist—I told ye nobody knows about them, didn't I tell ye that?

SOCRATES: Are you listenin' t'me—d'ye have any thoughts on shit like this—is it just me or we all like that or what? What d'ye think?

PETESY: Socrates, stop it, just fuckin' stop it—I have no room for this gear y'understan'—I've other stuff in my life to sort out— practical shit y'know, the real world, mortgages, bills, work, that world—understand. They don't exist right, all we gotta do is fire them into the back a the van.

SOCRATES: So that's it, nothin' else, that's it, all we're about is stealing tiles is it?

PETESY: Correctamundo—twenty minutes gets them into the back a the van, nobody's any the wiser.

SOCRATES: The real world, the practical world?

PETESY: Real—practical—yes.

SOCRATES: One a the plumbers got caught tea leafin' the other day—he's banjaxed, that practical enough?

PETESY: An' what?

SOCRATES: He's out, we get caught, we're out.

PETESY: I heard nothin' about that, what plumber?

SOCRATES: What plumber, what plumber, the plumber plumber.

PETESY: There's two plumbers.

SOCRATES: The big fat geezer.

PETESY: They're both big fat geezers.

SOCRATES: The one that kicked a hole in an Alsatian's throat—that one.

PETESY: A Doberman an' the fella ripped its lugs off.

SOCRATES: Ripped its lugs off—what for? You talk a lotta balls y'know that?

PETESY: Wasn't it goin' after one of his kids or somethin'—another thing too, it was a spark not a plumber—know the wee small one with the big napper an' the goat beard? Him.

SOCRATES: Him? Sure, he's not married.

PETESY: Maybe the dog was goin' for him then, I don't know.

SOCRATES: What would he rip the ears off it for?

PETESY: To fuckin' stop it.

SOCRATES: How would that stop it?

PETESY: Rippin' its lugs off wouldn't stop it?

SOCRATES: No—that just piss the dog off—kickin' a hole in its throat's a different matter, can't do any damage if it's a Chelsea boot stuck in its throat.

PETESY: That right—neither of the plumbers wear Chelsea boots, the spark does though.

SOCRATES: That's not right now 'cause they all wear trainers in case they get a shock.

PETESY: Ye couldn't kick a hole in a dog's throat if ye were wearin' trainers.

SOCRATES: Why not?

PETESY: Why not? What's wrong with you? Why not—'cause they're made for runnin' not kickin' holes in the throats a mad fuckin' dogs.

SOCRATES: Chelsea boots are, are they?

PETESY: Well there's certainly a bit more fuckin' wear an' tear in them isn't there.

SOCRATES: Kicked a hole in yer head.

PETESY: Doberman—no ears—spark.

SOCRATES: Whatever, fuck that—the fat plumber one with the beard.

PETESY: Him aye.

SOCRATES: Banjaxed.

PETESY: What's that gotta do with us?

SOCRATES: Heavy Hole'll be on the look out now.

PETESY: No delivery note—so they don't exist.

SOCRATES: They're not ours, know what I mean, they don't belong to us.

PETESY: Things that you tea leaf don't normally belong t'ye, else there'd be no point in fuckin' stealin' them.

SOCRATES: Aye but we know Heavy Hole, we know him—that makes it personal.

PETESY: Fuck Heavy Hole, what's he ever done for us?

SOCRATES: That's not the point.

PETESY: That's precisely the point. He ever invite ye up til his house—no. Ye ever go out for a swally with him—no. Ye on his Christmas card list—fuckin' no. We don't know him, he employs us, that's it. He's a businessman an' we graft for him, fuck all personal about that.

SOCRATES: What, that mean we're entitled t'steal off him?

PETESY: By the rules I live by, yes. He's a lot more than I'll ever have an' I helped him get it so fuck'im.

SOCRATES: Aye, I know fuck'im, but y'know what a mean, there's a principle involved here—like it or not he's part of our world isn't he, it be like stealin' from yer own—morally it's not right.

PETESY: Tell me this well—is it morally right that we only get paid enough readies—on purpose by the way, don't forget that, on purpose—that we only get paid enough readies to keep our heads a cuppla inches above the shit heap—is that morally right?

SOCRATES: Ye get paid the worth of what ye do—fuckin' market forces an' all that gear dictate that don't they—that's fuck all to do with Heavy Hole—economics, supply an' demand that's what that's all about.

PETESY: All them things are a con—they're there t'make sure that people who haven't a pot t'piss in remain without a pot t'piss in—I don't go by those rules, I go by rules that suit me, not someone else.

SOCRATES: It's difficult innit, makin' up yer mind about stuff—havin' problems about decidin' about things at the moment y'know.

PETESY: It's not life an' death shit, Socrates, we're only stealin' a pallet of fuckin' tiles. Heavy Hole's insured, we steal the tiles, he claims the readies back—what's fairer than that?

SOCRATES: That's true now, hadn't thought about that one, that illuminates the whole proceedin's a touch. What about the other two?

PETESY: Fuck'em.

SOCRATES: Fuck'em?

PETESY: Nothin' t'do with them. They're t'know nothin' about it, it's between me an' you.

SOCRATES: Just me an' you.

PETESY: Just me an' you—sixty-forty split.

SOCRATES: Sixty-forty?

PETESY: Aye—I get the biggest share 'cause it was my idea.

SOCRATES: How d'ye know I wasn't thinkin' about it?

PETESY: Didn't ye just give me all that right an' wrong shit.

SOCRATES: Might've been lyin', could've been thinkin' about it all along.

PETESY: Ye said fuck all well.

SOCRATES: I wanted t'see how the land lay—what yer tellin' me here is ye get extra readies for speakin'.

PETESY: How the fuckin' land lay? Right, alright, were you thinkin' about it?

SOCRATES: No.

PETESY: What the fuck then?

SOCRATES: Sixty-forty—if we're caught aren't we both goose an' ducked—so what's this sixty-forty business?

PETESY: Just for the sake of argument ye were thinkin' about it—ye didn't give it any of the verbals so there's no point in it. I though it an' spoke it, so I started the whole process off—that's why sixty-forty. Anyway it's me that has the contacts.

SOCRATES: Who?

PETESY: If I tell ye you'll know then.

SOCRATES: Correct—who?

PETESY: Jimmy Blow.

SOCRATES: Jimmy Blow, Jimmy fuckin' Blow—the whole site knows that.

PETESY: Aye but ye said fuck all. It's the same thing.

SOCRATES: Sixty-forty, behave yerself. [DING-DING *enters from the other room.*] That's not on y'know.

PETESY: Alright there Ding-Ding aye?

DING-DING: Aye. Need another pair of snips—spring's gone in mine.

PETESY: In the tool box.

SOCRATES: Sixty-fuckin'-forty.

PETESY: Sixty-forty, listen to him will ye. We're tryin' t'work out Ding-Ding what the percentage split would be between fruit an' sugar in a pot of jam—I reckon sixty-forty.

DING-DING: Sounds right to me.

SOCRATES: It's not well, I'm tellin ye it's not.

PETESY: Aye. Ye get the snips Ding-Ding?

DING-DING: Aye. Find the delivery note did ye?

PETESY: No—doesn't matter. I'll count the buckets or somethin'.

DING-DING: If ye come across it give us a shout.

PETESY: What for?

DING-DING: I wanna check somethin' on it.

PETESY: Check what?

DING-DING: Somethin'.

PETESY: Aye, but what?

DING-DING: Nothin'.

PETESY: Somethin'—nothin'—what?

DING-DING: I think we're a box of spacers short—if I had the note
I could check it y'know.

PETESY: If I come across it sure I'll fire it in til ye.

DING-DING: Aye. Sixty-forty sounds right t'me Socrates.

SOCRATES: Not in my book it's not.

PETESY: Cookbook Ding-Ding wha?

[DING-DING *exits to other room.*]

PETESY: What's wrong with you, they're not t'know nothin' about
this—say nothin'.

SOCRATES: I don't know about all this.

PETESY: Ye can't back out now it's all up an' runnin'.

SOCRATES: I didn't declare my hand either way—we're just talkin'—
all we're doin is talkin'.

PETESY: I can't do it on my swanny, it's a two man effort.

SOCRATES: A fifty-fifty effort.

PETESY: Puttin' me under pressure now.

SOCRATES: I'm just sayin' what's fair that's all.

PETESY: What's fair.

SOCRATES: Aye.

PETESY: Scrub it—forget it—we'll not do it—that's fair.

SOCRATES: Aye.

PETESY: Aye.

SOCRATES: Ye positive now—it's clear it's sorted out in yer head--
the war's over regardin' this.

PETESY: Not doin' it.

SOCRATES: I've a suggestion well.

PETESY: What?

SOCRATES: See the pallet a tiles out there nobody knows about, we'll
steal them.

PETESY: Away an' fuck.

SOCRATES: If we agree t'steal them I get a bigger whack 'cause it was
my idea.

PETESY: My idea.

SOCRATES: That was a different idea which you've just knocked on
the head—this is a new idea, my idea.

PETESY: Who's yer contact?

SOCRATES: Jimmy Blow.

PETESY: Fuck off.

SOCRATES: My idea, my contact, what's the problem.

PETESY: I need the readies.

SOCRATES: Who am I—the Aga Khan?

PETESY: I need it for somethin' definite—it's has t'be got. Everythin' else is shit right, forget about all that, this is the reason right.

SOCRATES: What, what is it?

PETESY: Ye gonna let me explain—this is personal shit. I don't like doin' this—I'm forcin' myself t'tell ye y'know.

SOCRATES: Welt away.

PETESY: Thank you.

SOCRATES: It's a pleasure.

PETESY: One a the kids, the eldest wee girl, really bright kid y'know, fuckin' frighten ye sometimes the crack she comes off with, intellectual gear I have problems gettin' my head round y'know, me an' her ma sittin' there half the time with blank coupins just listenin' til her—she's top trick in school an' all that business. Anyway her school's doing this exchange dixie, extended holiday type a thing t'France an' she's been picked t'go. There's grant money available from somewhere which is fine but you've gotta fork out a big whack of it yerself. The readies has t'be in next week—haven't got it, understan'? In a way I'm thinkin' fuck it it's only a holiday she doesn't go it's not the end a the world for her but in the backa my mind I keep thinkin' this is an opportunity for the kid—experience stuff I didn't experience, go t'places I've never been—somethin' might come of it y'know. All this shit here, it's good enough for me it's what I'm used to but if somethin' better can happen for her why shouldn't it happen an' even if it didn't it would be something' t'look back on y'know. That's it, that's the reason.

SOCRATES: I don't believe you just told me that.

PETESY: I didn't wanna say. Didn't I say I didn't wanna say?

SOCRATES: Ye fuckin' did though.

PETESY: No sixty-forty—fifty-fifty.

SOCRATES: Very good, that's very good Petesy.

PETESY: What?

SOCRATES: I take any type a cut I look like a complete bastard now don't I?

PETESY: Are ye in or out?.

SOCRATES: Hobson's fuckin' choice.

PETESY: Forget I told ye.

SOCRATES: Aye.

PETESY: I'm serious forget about it—yer either in or out.

SOCRATES: I say no you be happy with that?

PETESY: You say no, you say no—are you sayin' no?

SOCRATES: I'm not happy about this Petesy, emotional fuckin' blackmail y'know, I'm not happy about that—made me responsible for shit that I'm not responsible for.

PETESY: Responsible for fuck all—if ye don't wanna do it then don't do it—makin' me feel like I'm beggin' ye here—fuck off—my family, I'll look after them I don't need you or no other fucker. Emotional blackmail, a business deal that's what yer bein offered a fuckin' business deal. Don't think yer doing me any favours—it's a business deal an' nothin' else.

SOCRATES: Right, alright, sixty-forty.

PETESY: No fifty-fifty, I want fuck all from ye.

SOCRATES: I don't mind if—

PETESY: I don't give a fuck what ye mind—this is a business deal fifty-fifty or nothin'.

SOCRATES: Don't be gettin' all fuckin' heavy here.

PETESY: I'm not, I'm calm. Yes or no?

SOCRATES: Alright.

PETESY: Ye sure now?

SOCRATES: D'ye want me t'sign somethin'—I've said alright haven't I?

PETESY: Have t'be at lunchtime.

SOCRATES: Aye.

PETESY: Just need t'get ridda them other two—say we'll meet them

for a swally round the corner, celebrate Ding-Ding's good
night Irene trick.

SOCRATES: Aye.

PETESY: I take the wee lad roun' now clean the van get it ready.

SOCRATES: Aye.

PETESY: Everything sound?

SOCRATES: Aye.

PETESY: Bit silent on it y'know.

SOCRATES: I'm agreein' with ye—aye means I'm agreein' with ye.

PETESY: You be alright here on yer own get everythin' squared up?

SOCRATES: Aye.

PETESY: In the name of fuck. [*Enters other room*] You be alright on
your todd, Ding-Ding?

DING-DING: Aye.

PETESY: C'mon Randolph, me an' yous goin' t'clean the van out.

RANDOLPH: Why?.

PETESY: What does it matter to you why we're just doin' it—so
c'mon. Fancy a cuppla gargles at lunchtime, Ding-Ding, all
head roun' the corner bit of a celebration an' that.

DING-DING: Lunchtime?

PETESY: Aye.

DING-DING: I've a cuppla things t'get sorted out.

PETESY: Yer last day y'know, can't let it go without an oul swally an'
that.

DING-DING: We'll see.

PETESY: C'mon you.

[PETESY *and* RANDOLPH *exit to on site.*]

SOCRATES: No talk about nothin', just words, no talk. [*Makes an
attempt to go back to work*] I can't be arsed with all this. [*He enters
other room where* DING-DING *is working.*] Ye busy?

DING-DING: Enough t'keep me goin'.

SOCRATES: Aye.

[SOCRATES *sits down and watches* DING-DING *work.*]

DING-DING: Ye finished in there?

SOCRATES: Nah.

DING-DING: Much a do?

SOCRATES: Nah.

DING-DING: Adhesives shite, too dry—lyin' too long.

SOCRATES: D'ye ever cry, Ding-Ding, ye ever just sit down an' cry?

DING-DING: No.

SOCRATES: I did the other day—I worked somethin' out for myself an' 'cause I realised the truth about somethin' made me cry—it's like it had been there all along an' it was slowly workin' its way out y'know—somethin' locked inside me waitin' t'be worked out—d'ye ever get that, ever feel like there's shit locked away, deep down or whatever, tryin' t'bust out or somethin'.

DING-DING: No.

SOCRATES: It was to do with my da—him as a person, y'know—d'ye ever do that—think about what type of person yer da was really like y'know—try'n get rid a all that sentimental fuckin' gear an' just have a look—d'ye ever do that?

DING-DING: No—give us over them snips. [*He does.*]

SOCRATES: Everybody thought my da was a great fella y'know, a character—yer da's a character, always remember people sayin' that—dead now like—yer brown bread doesn't matter a fuck what ye were does it? Yer oul lad dead aye?

DING-DING: A lifetime—retirement fucked 'im.

SOCRATES: My oul lad was a hero t'me—when I was a kid I used t'think that if everybody respected me the way people respected my da that yer life would be worthwhile y'know, somethin' worth livin'. His funeral was fuckin' massive, all weepin'. 'There'll not be another one like yer da.' 'If yer half the man yer da was, you'll do alright son.' Ye never understand shit that's goin' on aroun' ye til after it's over, sure ye don't? Bright man, never made anything of himself y'know—spent all his life graftin', diggin', liftin', sweatin'—that fucked him up, took to the gargle an' that's when everybody thought he was a great fella—on Friday's I hadda go roun' t'the bar an' get money off him for my ma y'know—I can see him sittin' there, crowd roun' him, drink flyin' an' him holdin' court—used t'bring me into the middle of them y'know, 'cause I was his son that made me a great fella too—a hero, my hero. Y'know what I worked out Ding-Ding—the thing that made me cry—I worked out that there's difference between bein' a character and havin' character. My da was a small, insignificant little person, who gave a fuck about nobody but himself, he thought more about gettin' a slap on the back for bein' a great fella by some other useless fucker than he did about the people that should've mattered to him—his family, his wife, his kids. When I was fifteen he fucked off—gave me some bullshit speech about how his life was a failure an' how he was a burden on us all an' then he fucked off an' left me ma with five kids—still a character of course, still gettin' the slaps on the back—no bottle, the man had no fuckin' bottle—rather than live a decent life he wanted to be a character in a story—fuck'im.

[SOCRATES *cries, not openly but with resistance.* DING-DING *continues to work.* SOCRATES *stops crying. Silence.*]

SOCRATES: I'm sorry.

DING-DING: Aye.

SOCRATES: I'm sorry Ding-Ding. I'm sorry.

DING-DING: Aye. That United's a bad lot aren't they—watched 'em the other night gettin' fuckin' hammered they were, end up winnin' one t'nil—jammie bastards—other team must've hit the bar four times—wee lad rattled it from about thirty yards, like a fuckin' bullet it was, keeper didn't smell it—jammie bastards—ye see it, must've been thirty fuckin' yards.

SOCRATES: Nah.

DING-DING: Good game—jammie bastards, thirty yards like.

SOCRATES: Aye. Things happen in cycles like don't they—same shit keeps comin' roun' again an' again.

DING-DING: That's right—same match last year same shit happened—jammie bastards.

SOCRATES: I don't mean that, that's not what I'm talkin' about— why the fuck would I wanna talk about that?

DING-DING: What then?

SOCRATES: The same shit happens—my da fucks off—I end up fuckin' off—I haven't seen her or my wee lad for months now—that's what I'm talkin' about, that's what a mean.

DING-DING: Oh that—right.

SOCRATES: Aye, that—not whether some pimply gobbed, overpaid little runt can kick a fuckin' ball or not—that—my life—that.

DING-DING: Aye.

SOCRATES: I should go roun' an' see them, shouldn't a—what d'ye think, should I go round an' see them?

DING-DING: I don't know. When?

SOCRATES: Now, go roun' an' see them now, do it now.

DING-DING: Aye now, if it's in yer head do it now.

SOCRATES: Talk to them.

DING-DING: Aye, talk to them—stay there for a while, have lunch. I'll cover for ye.

SOCRATES: Maybe arrange t'bring them out for dinner or somethin'—bring them out tonight—just the three of us—talk to them.

DING-DING: I'll cover for ye—dinner tonight's a good idea.

SOCRATES: Ye say to Petesy—tell him, tell him I'll be back soon.

DING-DING: Never mind about that, fuck that, I'll sort that out.

SOCRATES: Aye now, now'd be the best time.

DING-DING: Aye.

[SOCRATES *exits to 'on site'. Moments later* PETESY *and* RANDOLPH *enter from 'on site'.*]

PETESY [*to* RANDOLPH]**:** Start sortin' out that crap in the corner. [*To* DING-DING] Where's 'heart on his sleeve' away—saw him beltin' out the gate there.

DING-DING: Away roun' t'see his fork an' knife an' wee lad.

PETESY: Ye serious?

DING-DING: His head's away—one minute he's slabberin' about his da or somethin' next thing he's up an' away—somethin' not right with him.

PETESY: He say how long like—what?—gonna be away long or what?

DING-DING: He just upt an' scarpered—I don't know.

PETESY: He said nothin'?

DING-DING: Somethin' about lunch.

PETESY: Back before lunch?

DING-DING: Gonna have lunch with them he said.

PETESY: Lunch when—lunch when we're havin' lunch—lunch then or lunch some other time?

DING-DING: Lunch he said—fuck, I don't know, ye eat lunch at lunchtime don't ye—talkin' about dinner as well.

PETESY: Not lunch then dinner—is that what he said, dinner?

DING-DING: Both—must be Hank Marvin.

PETESY: Let me get this straight here—he's not comin' back, that it?

DING-DING: Look Petesy, I don't know his head's gone—he's talkin' about his da then he's on about his fork an' knife an' wee lad, then he's talkin' about meals then he's up an' away.

PETESY: Fuck'im—said nothin' like just away—fuck'im.

DING-DING: There's somethin' not right with him I'm tellin' ye.

PETESY: I know that.

DING-DING: I'm graftin' away, he's spoutin' some cleavers in my ear about discoverin' somethin' about his da or somethin' next thing he's gurnin' away like a child—mad man, know what I'm sayin'—name of fuck ye can't be at that crack—that's not on, ye can't be at that.

PETESY: A know that, a know that—fuck'im.

DING-DING: All the years I've been graftin' never witnessed the like of that—I've seen men go through some serious shit but I mean it never got outta order—just burst into tears, I don't know what the fuck he was expectin' me t'do—not equipped to handle that gear like am a?

PETESY: Who the fuck is—he should know better like shouldn't he?

DING-DING: Correct—know better, that's right.

PETESY: You listenin' to this, Randolph, this is important, listen to what's bein' said here.

RANDOLPH: What?

PETESY: When yer workin' with other men right, in a situation like this, see all the emotional shit that ye get elsewhere, keep it til yerself 'cause once ye start givin' it the verbals yer napper goes—men yer workin' with don't want that—always gotta keep the napper straight.

DING-DING: Fuckin' embarrassin', that's what it is—embarrassin' other people yer are.

PETESY: Man's right—not only are ye fuckin' about with the relationships between you an' yer workmates yer embarrassin' people as well—first rule of work, if it's not within the chat that we work within' ye say fuck all, remember that—fuck all.

RANDOLPH: Got ye—fuck all.

DING-DING: Tried to steer him away from it too, havin' none of it he was—he's givin' it the weepin' trick I piped in with what ye think about the match the other night.

PETESY: That's a good one—sound bet—football's always a sound bet.

DING-DING: Fucker let on he hadn't seen the match.

PETESY: He had an opportunity, ye give him an opportunity?

DING-DING: Practically told me to shut up—fuckin' head's gone.

PETESY: A know that—see the one yer wee man hit from thirty, fuckin' doosey.

DING-DING: Jammie bastards, I kept sayin' that.

RANDOLPH: Same wee lad hit one like that the other week too.

DING-DING: A saw it—fuckin' belter.

PETESY: Hit them with both feet he can.

DING-DING: If they put that wee lad up for sale ye couldn't buy him—some a them third world chats wouldn't have enough national fuckin' income to pay for that wee lad.

PETESY: He's good.

DING-DING: Star he is.

PETESY: He's not comin' back then—fuck'im.

DING-DING: Lunchtime, after lunch—I don't know.

PETESY: Just up an' away—fuck'im—I'm away in here.

[PETESY *exits to other room.*]

RANDOLPH: I reckon ye get ten million for that wee lad—he'll not stay with them—that type of readies floatin' about—ye think he'll stay with them?

DING-DING: Don't give a fuck what he does son—that's Socrates away all we gotta do now is get rid of shit for brains.

RANDOLPH: Aye.

DING-DING: What was all that crack about cleanin' the van out?

RANDOLPH: Nothin' just said it looked like a shit heap.

DING-DING: Save us doin' it.

RANDOLPH: I did do it.

DING-DING: Save me doin' it.

RANDOLPH: Aye.

PETESY [*other room—thinking aloud*]: Swannin' off—no reason like—can't trust a man at that crack—can't say what he's thinkin'—fuck that. [*Pause*] Randolph, 'mere a minute.

RANDOLPH [*enters other room*]: What?

PETESY: Shut the door behind ye.

RANDOLPH: What?

PETESY: That cryin' trick fucked Ding-Ding up didn't it—he's alright Ding-Ding isn't he—sound man.

RANDOLPH: Aye.

PETESY: I was just thinkin' about somethin' there—just between me an' you now, understan'?

RANDOLPH: Aye.

PETESY: That's good—Socrates' a bit dodgy at the moment y'know— ye get the fellin' he'd drop tools an' do a bunk on ye if it suited him—that's not a good situation work wise an' with Ding-Ding packin' it in—it's all a bit up in the air y'know—could get somebody else in for Ding-Ding but then we mightn't hit if off with the guy or whatever y'know an' that would fuck the whole show up. Might be a better idea if you took over from Ding-Ding.

RANDOLPH: Ye serious—that'd be brilliant Petesy. I need the extra ... y'know an' that would help me—

PETESY: Slow down there Tonto, nothin's sorted yet—take two or three months but I could bend Heavy Hole's ear about it maybe speed the thing up—tell him yer sound, get him on yer side y'know—think that'd be a good idea, would you be up to it ye reckon?

RANDOLPH: Certainly, no sweat about it, Petesy. I'd be sound.

PETESY: Few extra shillins in yer sky rocket come the end of a week.

RANDOLPH: That'd be great—I'm savin' to buy a motorbike y'know—have t'put money away in a club an' that.

PETESY: Are ye, that's good. Extra responsibilities as I said—bit of decision makin'.

RANDOLPH: I can handle that.

PETESY: I think ye could.

RANDOLPH: When ye gonna say to Heavy Hole—soon like, next week or what—when ye sayin' til him?

PETESY: That depends on you.

RANDOLPH: What way?

PETESY: Fuck all for fuck all—I do somethin' for you, you do somethin' for me.

RANDOLPH: What, anything, name it.

PETESY: Pallet a tiles lyin' out the front there, I want ye t'help me steal them.

RANDOLPH: Shit.

PETESY: There's nothing to it kid, just fire them into the back of the van at lunchtime, shift them, that's it.

RANDOLPH: Pallet a tiles roun' the front—lunchtime?

PETESY: Aye—fuck all to it plus there's a few quid there for ye.

RANDOLPH: Lunchtime.

PETESY: Friday lunchtime everyone fucks off—place til ourselves—happy days—tell the other two meet them roun' the bar for a swally—weigh in late.

RANDOLPH: What if I knock ye back?

PETESY: Ye gonna knock me back?

RANDOLPH: Don't know.

PETESY: Put it like this—no good word to Heavy Hole plus I can make life shit for ye.

RANDOLPH: You do that already.

PETESY: More shit then—I need ye t'do this for me.

RANDOLPH: Why?

PETESY: Got fuck all t'do with you why y'understand', nothin'—all you need know is I need someone t'give me a han' that's all, workmates helpin' each other out, isn't that the way the world should be.

RANDOLPH: Aye workmates helpin' each other out.

PETESY: Just look upon it as a business deal that works to both our benefits—you get what you want I get what I want, nobody's any the wiser, no harm done.

RANDOLPH: Aye.

PETESY: Away back in there give him a hand. Oul fucker probably sleepin' by now.

RANDOLPH: Aye.

PETESY: Ye get nothin' for nothin' kid.

RANDOLPH: Aye.

[RANDOLPH *enters other room.*]

DING-DING: What shit for brains want?

RANDOLPH: Nothin'.

DING-DING: Nothin'.

RANDOLPH: Aye, nothin'. [*Pause.* RANDOLPH *starts scratching his arms.*] Fuckin' arms goin' mad with itch.

DING-DING: Grout dust—drop a soap an' water sort that out.

RANDOLPH: I know what it is.

DING-DING: What?

RANDOLPH: I didn't want t'say anythin' to ye about it. [*His head starts to twitch.*] There's that away now too. [*Scratching—twitching—his body jerks.*] The jerkin' now—it only happens at certain times, it's stress related—first happened when we were kids, just about to raid an orky an' this started, first the scratching then the other gear.

DING-DING: I've heard of it [*Scratching*] it can be serious [*twitching, jerking*] has been know to stay with people for years.

RANDOLPH: Stop fuckin' about.

DING-DING: Maybe it's contagious.

RANDOLPH: The stress comes from a reaction to the notion of gettin' caught—my lamps will start to swell up soon then I go temporarily blind.

DING-DING [*stops*]: Nothing wrong with a bit of nerves Randolph son.

RANDOLPH: No joke.

DING-DING: Don't fuck me about—I told ye that.

RANDOLPH [*stops*]: We'll leave it til Monday, tiles still here then it's a bog cert they're nobody's.

DING-DING: This job's finished today, I'm leavin' today, we're doin' it today. [*Arm around* RANDOLPH'S *shoulder*] Think about the motorbike, ye see it, just you keep that picture in yer head.

RANDOLPH: But Ding-Ding it's not—

DING-DING [*pulls* RANDOLPH *close-tight*]: A commitment has been made there's nothing else to be said—[*Smiling*]—don't panic son, there's no need to panic.

RANDOLPH: I'm not, I'm not. I'm sound, just havin' a bit of a laugh y'know, just a bit of an oul laugh—ease the tension a bit Ding-Ding that's all—nothin' t'worry about where I'm concerned.

DING-DING: We're sound then.

RANDOLPH: Alright if I go for a dander for five minutes, just want to walk about the place, check everything's alright y'know.

DING-DING: You do that, you do that son.

[RANDOLPH *exits to 'on site'.*]

DING-DING: Temporary fuckin' blindness wha'?

[PETESY *working in one room* DING-DING *in the other. Socrates enters from 'on site' to room* DING-DING *is in.*]

SOCRATES: Thank you for covering for me, you are a man of good character, an outstanding and upstanding individual whose worth like all real martyrs will only be realised when you bite the big one and take your rightful place amongst the Gods.

DING-DING: I thought—

SOCRATES: Don't think, do—the foundation of all human endeavour.

[SOCRATES *exits to other room.*]

DING-DING: Fuck him.

PETESY: Where the fuck were you?

SOCRATES: This another lover's tiff honey—not jealous were you?

PETESY: Where were ye?

SOCRATES: I had an idea, a thought, I acted on it and from that some good has burst onto the scene, now the world's a happier place.

PETESY: Happier fuckin' place. Aye. Ding-Dings said you were away for lunch—lunch that's what he told me—just up'ed an' fucked off, that's what he said.

SOCRATES: Aren't I here now, had t'come back for the pilfering chats didn't a?

PETESY: I was thinkin' about that ... it might be better if—

SOCRATES: All systems are go—know what happened t'me there, something small but something good, which makes it probably something big, doesn't it?

PETESY: Socrates about the other thing, there's somethin'—

SOCRATES: Howl on a minute—this is important, I need to speak this out y'know—I'd worked out y'see that my da didn't treat his kids an' wife well an' it looked like I was goin' that way so I said fuck it I'm goin' roun' t'see them—bit iffy at the start so I thought I'll be honest here, fuck it I'll be honest—I'm confused I said, I'm lonely an' I just wanted t'see you an' the wee lad— she smiled—brilliant—first time I was ever honest with her an' she smiled—wanted t'bring the two a them out tonight for a meal, special dixie y'know just the three of us—just spendin' time together talkin' that's all—she wasn't keen on the idea— a smile doesn't wipe the past out I understand that—the wee lad says he wants t'go to the pictures—she says why don't you take him—I'm takin' my wee lad to the pictures tonight, him an' me a boys' night out—ye could see it in his smile—me an' my da are goin' to the pictures.

PETESY: Good—good—about this other thing.

SOCRATES: What?

PETESY: The tiles.

SOCRATES: Aye, everything's sound, lunchtime.

PETESY: I don't know, hearing about the plumber gettin' maclatched and that—it's thrown me a bit y'know.

SOCRATES: Fuck all t'do with us that's what ye said—you said that didn't ye?

PETESY: I know, I know that—it's just maybe this is a bad idea at the moment, maybe we should leave it for now y'know—let the dust settle, give it a few days.

SOCRATES: It's bein' done now we decided that, no need for any more thinkin' about it.

PETESY: I know what we decided—all I'm sayin' is it might be a bit dodgy.

SOCRATES: She says to me, in passin' like, that she was skint—I've been givin' her fuck all for a while y'know—I said til her, don't worry about that, that's alright, I'll get ye a chunk a readies— it has to be done, the woman has bills to pay an' shit y'know.

PETESY: Leave it til Monday, or later next week even, now seems like a bad time, that's all.

SOCRATES: I've already said—I've made a commitment here y'know, I can't go back on that—she's happy about the situation, understandin' what I'm sayin'.

PETESY: I'm just not sure.

SOCRATES: Fuck not bein' sure—ye put me in a corner earlier on— you were sure enough then.

PETESY: Put in fuck all corner. Ye made yer own decision, nothin' else involved there, nothin'.

SOCRATES: You were on ma back an' ye know it—made me feel like the wee girls trip an' everythin' was beat out if I didn't come on board.

PETESY: A business deal that's all, I don't wanna hear anything about that—I said t'ye an' that's it.

SOCRATES: Ye gonna let me speak here. I've somethin' t'say y'know.

PETESY: Don't be gettin' all fuckin'—

SOCRATES: Can I speak here? [*Pause*] You had yer reasons, ye told me them, I understood they were important t'ye so instead of

tellin' ye t'go an' fuck yourself I came on board—all I'm doin'
now is the same thing I'm tellin you this is important to me—
it's not just doin' somethin' 'cause it's there t'be done—there's
a reason an' the readies are important to me.

[RANDOLPH *enters from 'on site'.*]

RANDOLPH: Is there any chance—

SOCRATES: We're talkin' here Randolph.

RANDOLPH: I just wanted t'see if—

SOCRATES: I don't give a fuck what ye want, I've told ye, we're talkin'
here—go in with Ding-Ding, whenever we're finished you can
do all the talkin' ye want—go on—go.

[RANDOLPH *exits to other room.*]

SOCRATES: Y'understand what I'm sayin' here—you asked me to do
somethin' an' I went along with it now I'm askin' you to do
something an' I want you t'go along with it.

PETESY: Right.

SOCRATES: Right what?

PETESY: Right, right.

SOCRATES: Good. I'm just gonna nip out an' get some flowers—be
a nice gesture that, wouldn't it—a nice gesture.

PETESY: Be a nice gesture t'do some tilin'—I think that would be
a nice gesture.

SOCRATES: It's nearly lunchtime aren't ye only gonna sweep up.

PETESY: I was but if yer doin' fuck all I'm doin' fuck all.

SOCRATES: Whatever—I've a good feelin' about today feels like the
start of somethin'—somethin' different, I don't know.

[SOCRATES *exits to 'on site'.*]

PETESY: Fuck it.

[DING-DING *and* RANDOLPH *in other room.*]

DING-DING: Did ye count them then?

RANDOLPH: No.

DING-DING: No?

RANDOLPH: Aye. No.

DING-DING: Why didn't ye count them?

RANDOLPH: Ye never mentioned countin' them.

DING-DING: Be a handy piece a information t'know.

RANDOLPH: Aye.

DING-DING: I'll do it willa—seein' it needs t'be done an' you didn't do it.

RANDOLPH: Aye.

DING-DING: Might nip roun' an' see if I can get yer man about the George Formby dixie.

RANDOLPH: What?

DING-DING: 'When I'm cleanin' ... ' forget it.

RANDOLPH: Aye.

[DING-DING *exits to 'on site'.* SOCRATES *enters other room from 'on site' carrying a bunch of flowers.*]

SOCRATES: Smell them, fill yer snazzle with that aroma.

PETESY: Aye, lovely.

SOCRATES: From now on any job we're on all bring in a bunch of flowers, put them in vase chats, leave'em about the place—instead of all this buildin', concrete shit, bitta colour about the place.

PETESY: Aye.

SOCRATES: I'm tellin' ye—whenever ye feel a bit dankers an' that have a butchers at the flowers then go over an' snort their beauty up intil yer napper make ye feel at one with the universe, make ye feel glad to be alive boy.

PETESY: Ye reckon?

SOCRATES: A do. What's the crack here—lunchtime—sit around for a few minutes, get them out t'fuck, go an' do the business, meet them roun' for a swally.

PETESY: Aye.

[DING-DING *enters other room from 'on site'.*]

DING-DING: A hundred and forty four boxes—plenty—got that other chat sorted out too, wee man's happy enough, drop him roun' the readies over the weekend—fucked he is, hadda get him up outta his scratcher, no life for a person that. Go in here, chew the fat with these two, get them outta the road, do what we have t'do, meet up with them later for a swally.

RANDOLPH: Aye.

PETESY [*from the other room*]: Nose bag time.

> [RANDOLPH *AND* DING-DING *enter other room. There are four buckets turned upside down. They sit and have tea from a flask—mid-conversation.*]

PETESY: That's what ye said, ye said that, didn't he say that, ye said everythin'.

DING-DING: Ye did, ye said everythin'.

SOCRATES: Aye an' what?

PETESY: No, I'm not havin' that—there must be some kindda dividin' line, some type of demarcation y'know.

DING-DING: Man's right 'cause somebody says somethin' doesn't make it true—it's like yer man in the paper, that geezer who put the dead sheep or somethin' in that glass tank chat.

PETESY: Hirst.

DING-DING: Aye him—that's not art, no matter what that fucker says t'me it's not art.

SOCRATES: That's my point if ye accept any of it ye have to accept the lot of it.

RANDOLPH: That wall that we've tiled, ship it over to the Tate, aye.

SOCRATES: Ye could aye, why not?

PETESY: Right howl on here—say a person makes their own clothes.

SOCRATES: That's art, do ye not think that's art?

PETESY: Ye gonna let me finish, ye never let anyone finish. A person makes their own clothes—they have t'wash them don't they, nobody wants glad rags, art or otherwise, that are fuckin' Abraham Lincoln—they wash them an' they put them on the line—no better still they wash them, it's rainin' outside so they hang them on the radiator t'dry—you go roun' to their house t'visit an ye see the clothes dryin', is that an exhibition?

SOCRATES: Clothes are meant t'be worn aren't they—anyway if they hang them for a purpose yes.

PETESY: Bollicks—and they were hung for a purpose—t'dry.

DING-DING: Socrates that purpose chat doesn't matter, 'cause the person lookin' at the them doesn't know what the crack is.

SOCRATES: What's that gotta do with it, it's the person who's hangin' them not the one lookin' at them.

DING-DING: On the way roun' to the house ye get soaked—ye take yer clothes off, hang them beside the other ones—somebody else comes in, has a jeff juke at the radiator—are yer clothes part of a exhibition now?

SOCRATES: I didn't make my clothes.

DING-DING: Same crack as before, they don't know that.

RANDOLPH [*to* PETESY]: Lend us yer cup.

PETESY: No.

SOCRATES [*to* DING-DING]: What does that matter?

DING-DING: Petesy said it earlier on—art an' all that fuckin' gear has t'do with the geezer lookin' at it not with the geezer who made it.

PETESY: Correct. Thank you Ding-Ding.

SOCRATES: It's one a them unanswerable ones like innit?

PETESY: How's it unanswerable if we've answered it?

RANDOLPH [*to* PETESY]: You've finished yer tea, lend us yer cup?

PETESY: No, I keep tellin' ye this, no.

RANDOLPH: Yer finished.

PETESY: Is he deaf? Are you deaf?

SOCRATES: Give the wee lad the cup, fella's allowed a mouthful a tea.

PETESY: No, he does this all the time, no.

RANDOLPH: Do what all the time?

PETESY: Where's yer own cup?

RANDOLPH: Why ye askin' that for, why's he askin' that—I don't have a cup, y'know I don't have a cup.

SOCRATES: It's unanswerable—it is—it's unanswerable.

PETESY: Me an' Ding-Ding wouldn't be allowed t'get it right sure we wouldn't.

DING-DING: We answer the unanswerable—that's us.

RANDOLPH: Am I invisible here?

PETESY: Might as well be yer not gettin the fuckin' cup—this is my cup where's yer cup?

RANDOLPH: I don't have a cup.

SOCRATES: Petesy just give him the fuckin' cup.

PETESY: Give him yers.

SOCRATES: I'm not finished, yer finished, give him the cup.

PETESY: No—he has t'learn this is work, he's responsible for his own stuff—not havin' his own cup means he's not takin' the thing seriously.

SOCRATES: Takin' what seriously?

PETESY: Work.

SOCRATES: He doesn't take work seriously 'cause he doesn't bring a cup?

PETESY: Not any cup, his own cup—an' yes.

RANDOLPH: I don't want yer cup, stick it.

PETESY: A will.

SOCRATES: I don't understan' that—a cup like.

PETESY: Ye don't understand what?

SOCRATES: Yer argument—the thinkin' behind what yer sayin', it's all up the fuckin' left.

PETESY: What, there can't be logic to normal things like, we can't have our own logic no—you only understand the logic of the loftier, head firmly up yer jam roll world? We're not allowed logic?

SOCRATES: Settle yerself.

PETESY: Aye a know but a mean it's not always up there some of it's down fuckin' here y'know.

DING-DING: Ye can have my cup.

RANDOLPH: Yer cup?

PETESY [*to* DING-DING]: Yer gonna lend him yer cup.

SOCRATES: No one touches yer cup—it's a rule—we all thought the thing must've been handed down t'ye from Moses.

DING-DING [*to* RANDOLPH]: Do ye want a cup of tea or not?

RANDOLPH: Aye, but there's no way I'm usin' yer cup, that's the cup, ye don't touch the cup even I know that, say I broke it—I don't want a lend of it, no.

DING-DING: I'm not lending ye it. I'm givin' ye it.

SOCRATES: Yer frightenin' us Ding-Ding.

PETESY: Yer givin' him yer cup, the cup that no one can touch.

DING-DING: When I first started I bought the cup now I'm leavin' might as well give it to the wee lad.

SOCRATES: Yer passin' him on a cup?

RANDOLPH: Yer passin' me on a cup?

DING-DING: Aye.

RANDOLPH: What am I gonna do with it?

DING-DING: Drink yer fuckin' tea outta it.

RANDOLPH: No, that's serious shit that, like puttin' a curse on me.

DING-DING: It's only a cup.

RANDOLPH: It's not, it's the cup—it's Ding-Ding's cup—a workin' man's cup, all that gear—couldn't drink outta that.

DING-DING: Suit yerself.

SOCRATES: Use mine.

RANDOLPH: Fill it up there. [*To* PETESY] What?

PETESY: No tea left.

SOCRATES: Time for a swally anyway.

DING-DING: We headin' roun' aye.

PETESY: Aye.

RANDOLPH: Headin' roun'?

  [*No one moves.*]

DING-DING: Sure Petesy why don't you an' Socrates welt on roun' there—we'll meet ye for a swally later.

PETESY: Meet us?

DING-DING: Aye me an' Randolph has somethin' t'sort out.

PETESY: What?

DING-DING: What?

PETESY: Aye what?

DING-DING: What—funny as fuck sometimes the way ye just forget somethin' when somebody asks ye—the head's a weird fuckin' gadget like innit. Randolph what is it—it's just not comin' t'me, can you remember.

RANDOLPH: No.

DING-DING: No?

RANDOLPH: No.

PETESY: Can't be too important can it?

DING-DING: Important alright—I have to ah ... have t'let the, let the dog out—the dog has t'get out y'know.

SOCRATES: What dog—you don't have a dog.

DING-DING: I don't, no that's right—the wee woman beside me though—wee woman beside me has a dog, she's away—I told her I'd do the business y'know—bring the wee lad with me y'know.

SOCRATES: Bring him? What for?

DING-DING: Big fuckin' dog, huge big fucker—take the two of us y'know big beast of a thing.

RANDOLPH: Sure why don't me an' Petesy meet ye's roun' there an' Socrates can go roun' with ye and let the dog out—Socrates likes dogs.

SOCRATES: I like dogs?

RANDOLPH: Aye—yer always talkin' about them aren't ye?

SOCRATES: No—hate the fuckers, hate all animals.

RANDOLPH: I thought you like dogs—sure yous two go roun' anyway—didn't ye want me for somethin', Petesy?

DING-DING: Socrates can't go, the dog'll do its nut.

SOCRATES: I'm not goin' anywhere—why would the dog do its nut?

DING-DING: Funny fuckin' animal.

RANDOLPH: Haven't me an' you t'sort somethin' out Petesy—a tile slipped or somethin' roun' the other room?

PETESY: That's alright I sorted that out.

SOCRATES: Sure the dog wouldn't know me.

DING-DING: That's it ye see hates people he doesn't know—anti-social bastard.

RANDOLPH: It's something else then, it's not that—what is it Petesy, somethin' else isn't it?

PETESY: No nothin' else.

SOCRATES: Do you know the dog Randolph?

RANDOLPH: What dog?

SOCRATES: The fuckin' dog.

RANDOLPH: No—are ye sure Petesy?

PETESY: Positive.

RANDOLPH: Right—that dog, Ding-Ding's dog, aye I know that one—big fuckin' dog that—I'll go roun' with ye Ding-Ding give ye a hand will a?

DING-DING: Yer comin' roun' t'help me with the dog?

RANDOLPH: Oh aye.

DING-DING: Sure about that?

RANDOLPH: Must be starvin' by now.

DING-DING: Hank Marvin. So we'll meet yous two roun' there then?

SOCRATES: Aye.

PETESY: Aye.

DING-DING: An' what, are yous headin' roun' there now or what?

PETESY: Hang on here for a while—[*To* SOCRATES]—you wanna hang on here for a while.

SOCRATES: Hang aroun' for a while aye.

DING-DING: Welt roun' now an' get a seat for us all—don't wanna be standin', fuck that caper—we don't wanna be standin'.

PETESY: Place is empty, it's always empty.

DING-DING: Aye that place, that place is empty—we're not goin' there, goin' roun' to the other place.

SOCRATES: Other place'll be bunged.

DING-DING: That's why I'm sayin' t'welt roun' now an' get a seat.

PETESY: I'm not goin' there—what would ye want t'go there for, ye can't get movin' innit—ye hate that place anyway, always sayin' it's full a shite hawks.

DING-DING: I thought'd be nice today—last day, celebration, bit more up market y'know.

PETESY: Up market, fuck that.

SOCRATES: Aye fuck that.

DING-DING: What one do you wanna go to Randolph?

RANDOLPH: The one ye need t'rush roun' now an' get a seat in.

PETESY [*to* DING-DING]: Is that where you wanna go?

DING-DING: Aye, be better, fuck that other place.

PETESY: We'll go there then.

DING-DING: Yous better motor then—get a good seat, one near the winda.

SOCRATES: All the seats be away by now. [*To* PETESY] All be away by now.

PETESY: Long ago—ye couldn't get a seat in it now for love nor money.

DING-DING: I'm tellin' ye welt roun' ye will.

PETESY: All gone now—we'll stand sure—I don't mind standin'. [*To* SOCRATES] D'you mind standin'?

SOCRATES: No—standin's alright.

DING-DING: I'm not standin'.

PETESY: Go to the normal place then.

DING-DING: Aye—other place is a fuckin' kip anyway.

SOCRATES: Thought it was up market.

DING-DING: It's a fuckin' kip.

PETESY: So we'll see yous roun' there then—better pints anyway.

RANDOLPH: Yous headin' now?

SOCRATES: Too early.

DING-DING: You'll miss the stew.

PETESY: Fuck the stew.

SOCRATES: Better get roun' an' sort that dog out, have it's own leg chewed off by now.

DING-DING: Fuck the dog.

SOCRATES: Ye can't leave it with no grub.

DING-DING: What d'you care? Sure you hate animals, nature all that shite.

SOCRATES: I know that but I wouldn't leave a dog with no grub.

DING-DING: Fuck the dog.

PETESY: Not goin' roun' then.

DING-DING: I just said fuck the dog, fuck the dog means I'm not goin' roun'.

PETESY: The two a yous headin' on roun' then—roun' to the other place.

DING-DING: No.

SOCRATES: You'll miss the stew.

DING-DING: I don't like stew.

SOCRATES: I've seen ye eat stew before.

DING-DING: No ye haven't.

SOCRATES: I have.

PETESY: I've seen ye.

RANDOLPH: So have I.

DING-DING [*to* RANDOLPH]: You've seen me eat stew have ye?

RANDOLPH: Thought I did—must've been ... soup—what was it, soup?

DING-DING: Aye, soup—an' that's shite roun' there too.

SOCRATES: Food is shit roun' there.

PETESY: Good pints though.

RANDOLPH: They do, they do good pints.

DING-DING: Aye.

PETESY: Just sit here for a while then.

DING-DING: Looks like it.

[*They sit in silence.*]

DING-DING: The notion for a gargle's wore off me.

RANDOLPH: Me too.

DING-DING: If yous two wanna—

PETESY: I'm not that keen myself.

DING-DING: Aye.

[*They sit in silence.*]

DING-DING: Ye sure now, I don't mind like, I know it's my leavin' dixie an' that but I mean if yous wanna welt on that's alright.

PETESY: Nah, I couldn't be arsed now.

[*They sit in silence.*]

SOCRATES: Fuck this—there's a problem here that needs to be solved—honesty, that's the thing—honesty.

PETESY: Socrates.

SOCRATES: It's alright, it's sound—my experience today has taught me that the only truth that the ... that the best way forward in any situation is to open yerself up—to be honest.

PETESY: Sure about that?

SOCRATES: Hundred percent—because of circumstances outside

our normal work situation Petesy and I have been forced into
a situation we would not normally find ourselves in—the role
of tea leafs—there's a pallet of tiles outside that we have
planned to steal. I now realise that not letting you two know our
plans was a mistake and I apologise as workmates and people
we have known for some time we should've treated you better
and informed you of what we were planning to do—which is
what I am doing now. [*Pause*] So as this operation needs to be
completed during lunchtime Petesy and I will now take our
leave to do the dirty deed unless of course you have something
to say about the situation in which case I would appreciate it if
you would keep your comments brief as time is of the essence.

PETESY: [*applauding*]: Yer good, yer very good. I have something
t'say.

SOCRATES: You do?

PETESY: Oh yes—where the fuck do you get off telling people my
business—who the fuck give you permission t'speak on my
behalf?

SOCRATES: I thought—

PETESY: Ye didn't think, what ye did was open yer gub an' speak—
the one thing ye didn't do was fuckin' think.

DING-DING: May I intervene in this spirit of openness?

PETESY: Oh fuck aye, intervene away.

RANDOLPH: Ding-Ding I don't—

DING-DING: I'm speakin' for both of us, this situation involves us an'
what I'm doin' is speakin' for us, understan'?

PETESY: What?

DING-DING: Me an' the wee lad had planned t'steal the tiles too.

PETESY: You an' him?

DING-DING: Didn't I just say that?

SOCRATES: This is good, I like this—ye see now if we hadda been up
front about this the situation—

PETESY: Shut up a minute.

SOCRATES: I'm just sayin'—

PETESY: Keep quiet—stop talkin' a minute. You an' him—when

did you an' him decide this?

DING-DING: What does that matter?

PETESY: When?

DING-DING: This mornin'—not that that's got fuck all t'do with you.

[PETESY *hits* RANDOLPH. SOCRATES *and* DING-DING *restrain him.*]

SOCRATES: What the fuck are you at?

PETESY: Let fuckin' go a me, let go.

DING-DING: What ye hit him for, he's a wee lad, what ye hit him for?

PETESY: I don't like being made a fucker of—let go a me, let fuckin' go.

DING-DING: Ye gonna calm down.

PETESY: I'm calm, I'm sound, just let go.

[*They let go.*]

SOCRATES: Ye sound?

PETESY: I'm sound.

SOCRATES: You alright, kid? [*To* PETESY] What the fuck you at?

PETESY [*to* RANDOLPH]**:** There was a problem ye should've fuckin' said, stood up like a man an' said face to face—I'm there tryin' t'do the right think by ye, yer makin' a fuckin' eejit outta me— ye had somethin' t'say ye should a fuckin' said it—fucker ye.

[RANDOLPH *lifts a hammer.*]

DING-DING: Yer outta order put the hammer down.

PETESY: What ye gonna do with that, ye gonna fuckin' use it?

RANDOLPH: C'mon, c'mon—I'll put it through yer fuckin' face.

DING-DING: Yer on yer own kid—there's rules y'know, there's rules, ye lift a hammer yer on yer own.

RANDOLPH: Fuck him.

SOCRATES: We gonna calm down here a minute.

PETESY: Ye gonna use that—c'mon, ye wanna use it, fuckin' use it c'mon.

SOCRATES: Calm down will ye.

PETESY: Fuck up, nothin' t'do with you, so fuck up.

SOCRATES: Ye gonna start on me now.

PETESY: If that's what ye want.

SOCRATES: Up to yerself—ye wanna go that way we can go that way.

RANDOLPH: Ye can't treat me like shit, ye hear me, ye can't treat me like fuckin' shit [*To* PETESY] Fuck you an' the tiles, fuck you.

DING-DING: What's he gotta do with you an' the tiles?

RANDOLPH [*to* DING-DING]: Fuck you too—wanna grab me by the throat now—ye wanna have a go at that now do ye—fuck the two of yous.

SOCRATES: What's goin' on here?

RANDOLPH: The two a them—don't say that, don't say this, just me an' you, just me an' you, I'm stuck in the middle—doin' me a favour? Fuckin' usin' me.

SOCRATES [*to* PETESY]: You ask him?

PETESY [*to* RANDOLPH]: Ye hadda spoke yer mind situation wouldn't a come up.

DING-DING [*to* RANDOLPH]: You agreed with him after you agreed with me?

SOCRATES: You ask him?

PETESY: Aye, I asked him.

RANDOLPH: He thinks yer fuckin' crazy—that's why he asked me, you can't be trusted yer fuckin' crazy.

SOCRATES: You say that?

DING-DING [*to* RANDOLPH]: Ye wee bastard, ye ungrateful wee bastard.

RANDOLPH: Lookin' after yer fuckin' self that's what you were doin'.

SOCRATES [*to* RANDOLPH]: Shut up—fuck you an' fuck him. [*To* PETESY] Did you say I was crazy?

PETESY: Ye are fuckin' crazy—talkin' a lotta shite all the time—yer fuckin' head's away with it.

DING-DING [*to* SOCRATES]: What you just say to me there?

SOCRATES [*to* DING-DING]: Fuck you, you heard, fuck you—I'm not interested in anythin' to do with you alright—fuck you.

[DING-DING *grabs* SOCRATES *by the jumper.*]

SOCRATES: Get yer hand off me. [*To Petesy*] I was just tellin' ye how I felt, what I was thinkin'—I'm not crazy.

PETESY: Yer fuckin' crazy.

DING-DING [*to* SOCRATES]: You don't talk to me like that.

SOCRATES [*to* DING-DING]: This is nothin' to do with you—I'm warnin' ye now get yer fuckin' hand away from me.

PETESY: Yer fuckin' crazy.

SOCRATES [*grabs* PETESY *by the jumper*]: Say it one more time I'm gonna put yer head through the wall.

PETESY [*grabs* SOCRATES *by the jumper*]: Any time yer ready fella, any fuckin' time.

[SOCRATES *breaks free.*]

SOCRATES: This is the wrong way t'go about this, we're goin' t'do it we'll do it fuckin' right. [*Moves to* RANDOLPH] Put the hammer down—nobody's gonna touch ye, just put the hammer down. [*Shouts*] Put it down. [RANDOLPH *puts the hammer down.*] We right now, we ready t'go. I hate work—I hate bein' here day in an' day out with you fuckers—I hate talkin' t'ye, I hate listenin' t'ye—I hate bein' in yer fuckin' company—yous are ruinin' my life an' I fuckin' hate ye's for it.

[*Silence*]

PETESY: I don't like doin' this.

SOCRATES: You rather we went to war?

PETESY [*to* SOCRATES]: Yer a whingin', gurnin' bastard—a wimp—a snivellin' poncy, cryin' fucker who makes the rest of us listen to the dribblin' shite that pours outta yer thin lipped, no backbone, whingy wee fuckin' mouth—I hate the sight of ye I'm ashamed t'be in the same room as ye—you other two, yer just lazy bastards.

[*Silence*]

RANDOLPH: I ... I ...

SOCRATES: Go ahead.

RANDOLPH: I look at you three an' all I see are three no good slabberin' fuckers who have done nothin' with their lives—ye's tell me what t'do an' none of ye's is worth spit—yous think yous are somethin' an' ye's are nothin', just three fuckin' tilers that have nothin', are goin' nowhere an' lead empty fuckin' lives.

[*Silence*]

SOCRATES: Ding-Ding. [*Silence*] Ding-Ding.

DING-DING: I don't give a fuck about any of ye's, yous mean nothin' t'me—I've spent most of my time with ye's an' yous mean nothin' t'me—I don't know who any of yous are. [*He takes a hanky from his pocket and wipes his eyes.*]

SOCRATES: That it—we finished?

PETESY: Looks like it.

SOCRATES: It's been said—it's done—back t'normal now right.

PETESY: Ye think so.

SOCRATES: Has t'be—this is our livelihood we have t'work together—it's as simple as that.

DING-DING: It's my last day.

SOCRATES: Have you somethin' t'say about that?

DING-DING: No.

SOCRATES: That's it finished then?

DING-DING: Finished.

[*They all sit in silence.*]

DING-DING: That United's a shower of jammie bastards aren't they?

PETESY: They've the referees bribed and everything for fuck sake.

SOCRATES: Stop talkin' nonsense.

DING-DING: Certainly they have.

RANDOLPH: I think they have.

[*The pallet of tiles is now on stage.* PETESY *and* SOCRATES *enter from 'on site' carrying two boxes of tiles each. They set them with the others.*]

SOCRATES: This is fuckin' stupid, we should've just fired them intil the van.

PETESY: They're better here—after work when the site's empty then we'll fire them intil the van.

SOCRATES: I can't be hangin' about here—ye understan' that, do whatever we have to do an' shoot the crow.

PETESY: It'll take as long as it takes.

SOCRATES: Can't be late for the wee lad, this pictures thing's important—can't be late, don't wanna be messin' the wee lad about—wanna show him I'm dependable—don't want him goin' through life thinkin' I'm lettin' him down all the time, that's all I'm sayin'.

PETESY: I wanna get home too y'know—sort this shit out then I can tell the wee girl I've got the readies for her for France—I wanna do that—I don't wanna be hangin' aroun' either.

SOCRATES: Ye get the readies tonight—if ye get it t'night I can give it til her t'night—wee lad to the pictures, give her the readies—it would help create a nice type of a feelin' about the place, y'know.

PETESY: Tonight's difficult, tomorrow.

SOCRATES: Tomorrow?

PETESY: Aye—Jimmy Blow be on the gargle tonight, have to be tomorrow.

SOCRATES: Positive now I can tell her it's on it's way.

PETESY: Aye tell her.

SOCRATES: Ye sure.

PETESY: I fuckin' said didn't a—didn't a just say it.

SOCRATES: Right. Know what the wee lad wants t'see, I thought this was fuckin' brilliant.

PETESY: What?

SOCRATES: *Thunderbirds*—when I was a kid I lived, breathed and shit that show—anything he wants t'know he just has t'ask his da—*Thunderbirds* was the business—*Thunderbirds are go*—only one I didn't reckon was Number 5—know that chat up in space—that wee lad never got home, I always felt that was a bit outta order.

PETESY: Did they not shift him aroun'—I thought they did—they did, they shifted him aroun'—a few episodes in space then back to the island for a rest, cuppla gargles, scratch his cleavers beside the pool.

SOCRATES: Alan ye called him.

PETESY: Aye.

SOCRATES: Ye reckon he got shore leave?

PETESY: Certainly he did.

SOCRATES: Might a done alright, makes sense like doesn't it—go ga-ga in space on yer lonesome.

PETESY: Aye.

SOCRATES: Could never work out that wee girl, know the wee ethnic minority chat, couldn't work out what the fuck she was at.

PETESY: She was the maid—wasn't she the maid—aye she was the maid.

SOCRATES: Maid—they had a fuckin' maid?

PETESY: Aye—she was always carryin' gargle aroun' on trays wasn't she—I always thought she was the maid.

SOCRATES: Adopted daughter maybe.

PETESY: She was a skivvy, they treated her like a skivvy, that means she was on the payroll—you adopt someone ye don't treat them like a skivvy do ye.

SOCRATES: That's true.

PETESY: I never liked that show anyway, *Joe Ninety* was a better show.

SOCRATES: Get t'fuck—Lady Penelope, Parker, that big pink fuckin' roller—behave yerself.

PETESY: *Joe Ninety.*

SOCRATES: Away an' fuck—Joe Ninety—puttin' them dopey testicles on him.

PETESY: Couldn't have been any dopier than the ones Brains wore—they had special powers, those blue chats had special powers—once he put them on an' got into that other chat, that spinnin' cage message, ye knew the world was a safe place—nobody fucked with Joe Ninety—wee lad used t'eat dynamite for fuck sake.

SOCRATES: Guff—fuckin' Nazi he was.

PETESY: Who?

SOCRATES: Blonde hair, blue eyes an' his granny was a German or somethin'—fuckin' Nazi.

PETESY: Behave yerself.

SOCRATES: Alright mightn't been a Nazi but he was definitely gay—never once saw him with a wee girl, not once.

PETESY: He was only a kid, what ye talkin' about gay—wee lad was savin' the world no time for that sexual chat anyway—*Thunderbirds*—heap a shite.

SOCRATES: Doesn't matter t'me one way or the other, just good t'be takin' the wee lad out that's all.

[RANDOLPH *enters carrying two boxes of tiles. Puts them with the rest.*]

SOCRATES [*to* RANDOLPH]: He thinks *Joe Ninety*'s better than *Thunderbirds*.

RANDOLPH: What's he talkin' about?

PETESY: Nothin'—shootin' the shit, passin' the time—nothin'—that the last a them?

RANDOLPH: Aye.

SOCRATES: *Joe Ninety*—yer fuckin' head's away with it.

PETESY [*to* RANDOLPH]: Ye sure now—none lyin' about out there, ye checked?

RANDOLPH: None lyin' about, I checked, that's the last a them.

SOCRATES [*looking at tiles*]: Doesn't look like much, does it?

PETESY: Looks like a pallet a tiles—what ye want it t'look like?

SOCRATES: I know it looks like a pallet a tiles—that's 'cause it is a pallet a tiles.

PETESY: Einstein.

SOCRATES: A mean the bit of hassle an' that it caused, doesn't look like much like.

PETESY: Look better if there were more of them that's true.

RANDOLPH: Doesn't matter what it looks like—gettin' us what we want innit?

PETESY: Shouldn't have t'fuckin' steal them t'get what ye want though should ye?

SOCRATES: Where's Ding-Ding?

RANDOLPH: Way roun' t'buy a bucket.

PETESY: Bucket a what?

RANDOLPH: Winda cleaner's bucket.

PETESY [*to* SOCRATES]: That's what we've t'work with. [*To* RANDOLPH] What the fuck are you talkin' about?   .

RANDOLPH: Did he not say t'ye?

PETESY: If he said would we be askin' ye?

RANDOLPH: I thought he said t'ye when we all agreed about the tiles an' that—did he not say?

PETESY: He didn't say.

RANDOLPH: That's what he's doin' with his share of the poppy.

SOCRATES: Buyin' buckets.

RANDOLPH: Winda cleanin'—some oul lad he knows, sellin' his round. Ding-Ding's buyin' it off him.

SOCRATES: Aye.

RANDOLPH: I'm tellin' ye, that's what he said—reckons it's gonna stop him from dyin' or somethin'.

SOCRATES: Winda cleanin' stop him from dyin'?

RANDOLPH: Somethin' like that.

SOCRATES: Winda cleanin'?

RANDOLPH: I'm only tellin' ye what the man said, I don't know, maybe he reckons winda cleaners don't die or somethin', I don't know.

PETESY: Fair play til him.

SOCRATES: Yer right fair play til him's right—winda cleanin' wouldn't be my preferred occupation—good luck til him though.

RANDOLPH: Somethin' wrong with his head.

SOCRATES: Nothin' wrong with his head—man's allowed t'work on, wants t'do that that's up t'himself—oh no, he's allowed t'do that.

PETESY: Man's showin' a bit of enterprise isn't he—nobody tellin' him what t'do, out on his own—that's alright, that's sound.

[DING-DING *enters from 'on site' carrying a bucket.*]

SOCRATES: Fuck, it's George Formby.

PETESY: When I'm cleaning dixies Ding-Ding wha—I've an oul shammie an' a string vest in the house, that type of object would be of use to you now I imagine.

DING-DING [*to* RANDOLPH]: That was nobody's business.

RANDOLPH: I thought you'd already said, I didn't know.

SOCRATES: No now Ding-Ding that's not right, don't be blamin' the wee lad here—we're allowed t'know that now c'mon til.

PETESY: If you were gonna say nothin' how were ye gonna explain the bucket?

DING-DING: Explain what, it's just a bucket.

PETESY: Ye buy them all the time do ye?

DING-DING: If ye hadda asked me about the bucket I'd have told ye to fuck off.

PETESY: That's lovely talk that from a winda cleaner—can ye picture him half-way up the ladder some wee woman says t'him 'want yer bucket filled mister'—away an' fuck yerself.

SOCRATES: Ye can't be at that now Ding-Ding, when yer a winda cleaner ye can't be talkin' like a tiler.

DING-DING: Away an' fuck yerself.

[PETESY *and* SOCRATES *laugh, then* RANDOLPH *and eventually* DING-DING.]

SOCRATES: What was that?

PETESY: That's tiler speak for thank you for expressing your opinion but on this occasion I feel I must beg to differ.

SOCRATES/PETESY: Away an' fuck yerself.

PETESY: 'Member the day we were standin' in the kitchen, wee woman says t'him [*indicates* DING-DING] "Do you think... [*laughter*] do you think the patterns should be randomised or uniform" ... how the fuck would I know?

[*They are all in a giggling fit.*]

SOCRATES: Wee woman says I don't think there's need for that language.

SOCRATES/PETESY: Away an' fuck yerself.

DING-DING: Oh aye, very good, aye a know.

SOCRATES: What about—attention.

DING-DING: 'Member that—she had lost it, something' not right with that wee woman's napper.

RANDOLPH: What, what was that?

PETESY: You not with us then, no.

SOCRATES: No, sure it must've been a good two years ago—wee woman we were workin' for had the hots for him [*indicates* DING-DING]—definitely some type a sexual thing goin' on.

DING-DING: That's not right now, don't listen t'him, that's not right.

PETESY: Didn't she keep givin' ye apples?

DING-DING: She wasn't right in the napper that's why.

PETESY: She didn't give me an' him any.

SOCRATES: She did not.

PETESY: She says to us, what's wrong with your friend he doesn't smile a lot, is he unhappy—Socrates says til her [*To* SOCRATES] what was it shrapnel, a bullet?

SOCRATES: No a metal plate in his head.

PETESY: Aye—he says that Ding-Ding suffered some serious shit durin' the war and he had t'get a metal plate in his head which was fuckin' him up.

SOCRATES: No, I said til her that yer head was divided intil a happy part an' a sad part an' the plate was stoppin' the blood gettin' t'his happy part—wee woman was away with the fairies like— this got her talkin' about the war an' she was askin' what battalion Ding-Ding was in.

RANDOLPH: You in the war?

DING-DING: No—fuck.

SOCRATES: Askin' a whole lotta stuff, so me an' him made it up, group squadron, fuck I don't know whatever it was—she was really gettin' intil it, she was in the army an' all. [*Starts giggling*]

PETESY: She left right, it was near lunchtime—we're in the bathroom or something [DING-DING's *giggling.*] talkin' away, bullshit, waitin' on lunch—she bursts in the door an' she had all the gear on her—her army uniform y'know—[*laughing*]—fuck—she had an apple in her hand for Ding-Ding—fuck—she shouted out, "Attention. Here's an apple for you soldier"—we're all lookin' at her, didn't know what t'say—lookin' at Ding-Ding—an apple for ye soldier—he says, "Put it on the plate." [*Laughter*] She salutes, marches over an' puts the apple on his head.

[*Mobile phone rings.* PETESY *answers it.*]

SOCRATES: William fuckin' Tell.

DING-DING: Attention soldier.

PETESY [*on phone*]: Yes John how are you no, no just a bit of a laugh aye oul story ... all red up aye, just about to ... aye ... what ... but ye can't ... I know ... John ye can't expect ... no ... I understand that, there's no need for ... right ... I understand that but Jesus

John ye know ... no I'm not ... no I'm not saying that, right ...
right ... that's extra ... yeah, aye ... It'll be ... finished yes ... he's
here do ye wanna ... no right ... aye right. [*Phone down*]

RANDOLPH: Attention.

PETESY: Fuck up.

SOCRATES: What?

[PETESY *walks to tiles puts his hand under the pallet. He takes out a
delivery note and hands it to* SOCRATES.]

SOCRATES: Deliver note—an' what?

PETESY: Ye not fuckin' read—the tiles are on it, can ye not see that,
it's fuckin' plain enough isn't it.

SOCRATES: The tiles are on it.

PETESY: Randolph go out to the van an' get the tool box back in.

SOCRATES: For what—what ye need the tool box for?

PETESY: To work, what d'ye normally fuckin' need it for?

SOCRATES: We're finished.

PETESY: The tiles are for here, there's another room t'be done an'
it's t'be done tonight. [*To* RANDOLPH] Did I tell you t'go an' do
something, well go an' fuckin' do it?

[RANDOLPH *exits to 'on site'.*]

SOCRATES: I don't get this, I don't understan'.

PETESY: Simple enough—we've more fuckin' work t'do, an' we're
gonna fuckin' do it—what the fuck don't ye understan' about
that?

SOCRATES: Ye didn't say anything to him, why didn't ye say anything
to him?

PETESY: Like what?

DING-DING: What room?

PETESY: What room what?

DING-DING: What room we workin' in?

PETESY: Room? One down the bottom a the corridor.

SOCRATES: Ye should've said somethin'.

[DING-DING *lifts two boxes of tiles and exits to 'on site'.*]

PETESY: We're doin' it, what else can I say?

SOCRATES: Tell him no.

PETESY: He'll get another squad in—that's us out.

SOCRATES: Fat bastard—he can't do that—fuck'im.

PETESY: He's done it—there is no 'he can't do that'—he's fuckin' done it.

SOCRATES: You should've said somethin'.

PETESY: Don't say that again—there was fuck all I could say, ye understan', fuck all.

[RANDOLPH *enters with tool box.*]

PETESY: Other room.

[RANDOLPH *exits to 'on site'.*]

SOCRATES: All night?

PETESY: Four or five hours I'd say.

SOCRATES: That's it like, ye make plans, have other business in the world t'sort out—all a that means fuck all though, work fucks all that up—yer told what t'do an' ye do it.

PETESY: It's no different for me, Socrates. I had plans too.

SOCRATES: Fuck'im.

PETESY: Correct.

SOCRATES: Four t'five hours?

PETESY: Aye.

SOCRATES: Positive?

PETESY: Aye.

SOCRATES: Have t'let the wee lad down—try t'make amends now I've t'fuckin' let him down again.

PETESY: Better start bringin' these roun' here—sooner we start sooner we're finished.

[*They lift two boxes of tiles each. Exiting to 'on site'* SOCRATES *stops. He puts the tiles back.*]

SOCRATES: I'm finished.

[RANDOLPH *enters from 'on site'*]

SOCRATES: I'm not doin' it—I've made my mind up, I'm not doin' it.

PETESY: Don't start Socrates, just lift the fuckin' things an' c'mon.

SOCRATES: No.

PETESY: I'm tired, I wanna get t'fuck outta here—can we just get this finished.

SOCRATES: No—there's more important things in the world than this—I'm bringin' the wee lad to the pictures—mightn't seem like much, mightn't seem important but that's what I'm doin'.

PETESY: Yer just gonna fuck off an' leave the rest of us—doesn't matter that it'll take us twice as long or fuck all—just you like, worry about gettin' yer world sorted out an' fuck the rest of us.

SOCRATES: You can do what ye want.

PETESY: No I can't, I've responsibilities, I need work, I need t'earn—that's what I have t'fuckin' do—there's no choice here.

SOCRATES: I'm bringin' the wee lad to the pictures.

PETESY: I'm not coverin' for ye, do whatever ye like but I'm not coverin' for ye an' if Heavy Hole asks me I'm tellin' him the truth, ye fucked off—he'll sack ye, ye know that.

SOCRATES: You do what ye have t'do, that's yer business, I'm just tellin' ye what I'm doin'. [*Puts his coat on and lifts the flowers.*]

PETESY: I'm not coverin' for ye.

SOCRATES: I'll maybe see ye on Monday.

[SOCRATES *exits 'on site'.*]

PETESY: You'll not be here on fuckin' Monday—queuing up at the fuckin' brew without a pot t'piss in that's where you'll be. [*Pause*] Bastard.

RANDOLPH: What we doin' about his overtime?

PETESY: What?

RANDOLPH: We could all do with the extra readies an' if we're doin' his work we should split the readies he was goin' t'get for it—fuck'em we've earned it, he hasn't.

PETESY: He gets whatever's due t'him for tonight plus we cover for him an' if Heavy Hole asks anythin' he went home sick.

RANDOLPH: But you just said—

PETESY: Doesn't matter what the fuck I said that's between me an' him—all you need to know is we're coverin' for him an' that's it.

RANDOLPH: Why?

PETESY: You know fuck all do ye—why?—'cause the fella's right that's why—he's doin' the right thing.

RANDOLPH: That's not right.

PETESY: That's what's happenin'.

RANDOLPH: I'm not doin' it.

PETESY [*up close to* RANDOLPH]: You do what I tell you t'fuckin' do—an' don't think I've forgotten what ye said earlier 'cause I haven't—goin' nowhere that what ye think—I'll tell ye somethin' kid yer gonna be the exact fuckin' same—start bringin' the tiles down to the other room.

[RANDOLPH *lifts two boxes of tiles and exits 'on site'.*]

PETESY [*on mobile phone*]: I'm gonna be late ... I just am that's why ... I'm workin'.

[*Empty wooden pallet on stage.* RANDOLPH *is sitting on pallet drinking tea and flicking through his magazine.* DING-DING *sleeping.*]

RANDOLPH: What d'ye think Ding-Ding red or black—I think black myself, there's somethin' classy about a black number, what ye reckon—a big black one that's what I reckon—wanna hear the shit I'd to take from Petesy there—fuck'im—no mention of the job either, that's that banjaxed—fuck'im—all I did was speak my mind like, that was the crack like wasn't't it—be like the rest of yous I don't think so, save the readies, get the bike I'm away. [*Accidentally knocks his tea over.*] Fuck that, I was enjoyin' that—have a wee sip of yers Ding-Ding wha'? You just sleep away there [*He drinks from* DING-DING'S *cup.*] Better sayin' fuck all like aren't ye, just keep yer nose down an' say fuck all—he's gonna give me a lotta shit like now—fuck'im—I'm goin roun' tomorrow an' joinin' that bikin' club effort, drop them a few shillins, fiver or somethin' that'll get the ball rollin'—pity there wasn't a window cleanin' club goin' you could have a crack at that Ding-Ding—it's fucked that like innit, thinkin' yer gettin' somethin' an' endin' up with fuck all—what about blue, aye blue be alright wouldn't it.

PETESY [*off-stage*]: Randolph c'mon til.

RANDOLPH: Right. Might say t'him about the job—aye—leave the

bikin' club thing until he gives me the wire about the job—
fuck'im—C'mon Ding-Ding son, sooner we get this finished,
sooner we get home.

[RANDOLPH *nudges* DING-DING. DING-DING *slumps over dead. Blackout.*]

DAMAGE DONE
(1994)

Damage Done has not previously been performed.

An ancient couple sit in armchairs, centre stage. They sit in silence.

HIM: What? Did you say something?

HER: No.

HIM: I thought I heard you say something.

HER: You're dreaming.

HIM: Aye. Maybe. [*Pause*] Maybe it was the last thing you said. [*Pause*] What was it?

HER: What?

HIM: The last thing you said.

HER: That was fifty years ago.

HIM: Doesn't time fly? [*Pause*] I suppose the cat's dead?

HER: We don't have a cat.

HIM: Must be dead then.

HER: We never had a cat.

HIM: Did we not? [*Pause*] It just shows you. I thought we did.

HER: It was a dog.

HIM: That's a strange thing for a cat to be—a dog.

HER: We had a dog.

HIM: I suppose the dog's dead then.

HER: I suppose so.

HIM: He never took his milk that dog. Do you ever remember ...

HER: Yes.

HIM: Do you ever remember ...

HER: Yes.

HIM: Do you ever remember the time we went to the pictures and saw a cowboy movie?

HER: No.

HIM: Neither do I. [*Pause*] Remember the dog though, bastard never took the milk.

HER: Language.

HIM: Aye. [*Pause*] The wee lad he'd be away too then would he?

HER: Dead.

HIM: He's away then. [*Pause*] Him and the dog.

HER: Do you remember ...

HIM: Aye.

HER: Do you remember ...

HIM: Aye.

HER: Do you remember the day we all went to the park, it was raining and we all got soaked?

HIM: No.

HER: Neither do I.

HIM: We should do this more often.

HER: What?

HIM: Yarn about the good old days. [*Pause*] I miss that.

HER: The times we had drivin' in that car, all of us in the car. [*Pause*] Chug, chug, chug.

HIM: We never had a car.

HER: We did.

HIM: It was a motor bike with one of those things stuck on it.

HER: What?

HIM: You know one of those things. [*Pause*] You know something stuck on it, a thing, like a funfair thing you sat in, on. A wee room. [*Pause*] One of those up and down and round and round. At the funfair.

HER: A wee room stuck to the motor bike.

HIM: Aye.

HER: I thought we had a car.

HIM: A wee car?

HER: Yes.

HIM: No.

HER: Yes.

HIM: No. A wee room like a wee car. [*Pause*] There's a name for those things. Bloody stupid thing.

HER: Language.

HIM: Oh shut up.

HER: Don't talk to me like that.

[*They remember. The following dialogue is said at speed.*]

HIM: You're always doin' that.

HER: And what about you?

HIM: I don't do that.

HER: No you do worse.

HIM: You do this every time we talk—spoil everything.

HER: Why's everything left up to me?

HIM: I do as much as you do.

HER: When have you ever done the ironing?

HIM: When have you ever put coal on the fire? Don't I make the dinner every day I come in from work.

HER: Big deal. When do you ever tidy up and do the washing? Have you ever cleaned the toilet? You pee all over the place too.

HIM: Here we go. Here we go, everything's my fault.

HER: What did you do today, after you made the dinner you sat in front of the TV and didn't move for the rest of the night.

HIM: I was tired. I had things on my mind.

HER: Do I not get tired, do I not have things on my mind? And then of course you have to have your wee drink because you're so stressed out.

HIM: Am I not allowed, have I not earned it? I need to get away from you for a few hours, bitchin' in my face all the time.

HER: Go on, away you go, why don't you go down to the bar and stand with all your mates, act the big lad, tell them all what a great fella you are.

HIM: [*Stands up*] Shut up I'm warning you, just shut up.

HER: [*Stands up*] You don't like hearing the truth do you, Jack the Lad.

HIM: I'm warning you, you're pushing me too far.

HER: What are you going to do big man, hit me again.

[*They stare at each other motionless then sit down. They sit in silence. Lights fade.*]

THE WAITING LIST
(1994)

The Waiting List was first performed at the Old Museum Arts Centre on 18th April 1994. The play was performed by Lalor Roddy. The production was directed by David Grant. Produced by Point Fields Theatre Company.

An empty stage except for the frame of a pram which the actor can use as he pleases. He should be in his mid-thirties and wearing either a dressing gown or pyjamas.

A big Sherman tank of a pram jammed against the front door—prams, to keep children in and bad boys out. They have a list, a shopping list for Taigs, Fenians, Popeheads, pan-nationalists, republicans, Catholics. Not two hundred yards and two weeks away this fella's in the sack with his girlfriend.

"Night night dear."

"Night night dear."

Door kicked in, bang, bang, bang, bang—end of story.

Now there's a list. And you never know I might be a desirable commodity, on sale as it were, lingering in the bargain basement so to speak. I'd rather be past my sell-by date but I'm not even half-way to my allotted three score and ten. Plus I'm not working at the moment which means your waiting time's doubled or seems like it 'cause I've nothing to do except paint the house a shitty yellow colour and push the youngsters, in the Sherman tank, through this mixed but not completely integrated area. Mixed only in the sense that I couldn't put a flag out or douse petrol over mountains of wood in the middle of the street and get a spark from two flints to make it whoosh, singing fuck this and fuck that, while scribbling down misspelt names on the back of a feg box with a well-chewed biro stolen from the bookies. Mixed in that sense. Not that I'd ever want to do those things, you understand, but you never know. That's the problem round here you never know—a wee bit of fear keeps you on your toes, never quite at ease, just slightly edgy. I could always ask I suppose. Next time I'm doing the shopping and

I see one of the lads poncing round Dunnes Stores with his dark glasses, pot belly, chunky gold jewellery, fat wife and snattery children.

"Excuse me, am I on your list? In between everything you need for an Ulster fry in one pack and a slimy bag of frozen chips—five per cent less fat of course. I would like to know, it would help me in my capacity as decision maker if I knew I was going to be around to view the consequences of my decisions."

"It's hard to say, kid," he whispers out the side of his mouth while one of his snattery, skinhead kids claws at his ma's taut bulging mini-skirt for a toy machine gun (they learn early) with real imitation bullets, flashing lights and noises, just like the one Rambo has sewn in between his muscular thighs, as he beats a track through the jungle, blasting the shit out of the dirty gooks.

"It's open season you see kid, it's difficult to tell. It's a lottery, your number's in the hat, what more can I say? After the shopping I always give her one on the sofa, do you wanna watch?"

So I'm waiting here, night after night, pram against the door, looking across the street to the house I was brought up in, thinking, musing, playing with the idea why would it be me? Am I on the list?

Tock-tick, tock-tick, tock-tick. Football in the entry, twenty aside, dogshit everywhere, use it for goal posts. I'm Geordie Best. Dribble, dribble, swerve, faint, swerve, dribble, dribble, looks up (sign of a good player—always looks up), whack and it rattles the net. The crowd go mad. *Geordie, Geordie, Geordie.* United 37, Chelsea 16. Stick insects, sliding in the shit and dreaming of Wembley (not Croke Park).

"Goal."
    "Offside."
    "Your ma."

"Aye, your ma."

Dawn to dusk. A big boy appears on the scene. Hair down to his arse, jeans up to his arse and boots gleaming—shined by his loving mother four times a day.

"He's a scout sent by Matt Busby. I've seen him in the park."

The stick insects gather round, ears pricked, eyes like saucers, minds agog.

"Are you a scout?"

"Aye sort of (ha, ha, ha). You, you and you."

Whisper, whisper.

"My da told me some guy gets over a hundred quid a week and he only plays for Spurs."

"Jesus."

"Bollocks."

"What'd he say?"

"Who you playing for?"

"Will your ma let you go?"

"Fuck up, Fenian bastard."

Smack smack kick kick. A bloody nose and me Geordie Best too. Football jerseys off, tartan scarves on. McDonald, McDougall, McClaymore, McKingbilly, the clan of Robbie Burns, who gives a fuck. And me I'm still Geordie boy and sure a good kicking never does you any harm anyway. Demarcation lines are drawn, whatever they are.

"Don't go here, don't go there, watch who you play with, be in before dark."

Father—"The boy should take up boxing, good clean sport. Discipline the mind, defend yourself." Mother—"It'll ruin his good looks, look at your fid you ugly wee bugger."

High cheek bones, I should have been a movie star but was never spotted, not by anyone from Hollywood anyway. Just keep playing and it'll all go away that's the trick. Failed the quallie that year, couldn't believe it, Einstein I was. Got a bike for being a failure. A Gobi Desert summer, Ulster '71 in full swing, dodgems, helter skelter, waltzers, big wheel—a quick thrill to unite the warring tribes. I'm on my bike, peddle, peddle, peddle, everywhere, everyday. After Wembley that big race in France was getting a turn. Three of us this day, a biking gang, the ton-up boys, get lost and end up in some 'get a damp, cockroach infested flat on the l9th floor with your demob suit' estate. Not like the entry, no dog shit anywhere—a bit of greenery and a playground. Swings, see-saw, roundabout, climbing frame, all good stuff—the ton-up boys.

"Where you from?"

"What school do you go to?"

"What football team do you support?"

"Say the alphabet."

"Sing 'The Sash'."

Should have taken up boxing, looks as if the cheek bones are going to get a burl anyway.

"Push faster, faster, faster. Faster you Fenian bastard. Need a rest, sit on the grass. Feel your mate's dick."

Smack.

"Feel it, you fruity fucker. This one's a fruit and a Fenian."

Punch. Dr. Martens. Kick kick kick—children can be cruel bastards, they're like adults that way. I'm starting to get the hang of this now. I'm a Taig and they're Orangemen—what could be simpler? Things are starting to hot up, houses and petrol bombs, hand in hand, made for each other. There's nothing like a bit of heat on a cold night when you're watching *Crossroads*. A mate of mine left his dog to guard the house—*whoof*. The Orangemen called him hot-dog, made him crazy. Nothing like a bit of humour. The parish priest after having a yarn with the Almighty formed a 'Stop Dogs Going Whoof in the Dark of Night Vigilante Group'. Patrolling the streets with hurls and bin lids. All dogs can sleep safe in their kennels, it's their owners who do the tossing and turning. Myself, I'm doing a bit more of the former than the latter.

"There's a wee girl, fancies you, she's a Protestant."

"What do you think, lads?"

"Get in there, you're a cert thing."

"All Orangewomen do it."

"Do you see the diddies on her, she didn't get them sitting by the fire."

Seven o'clock next night up the entry. Find a patch with no patch shit—ha, ha. Talk talk talk lumber lumber lumber feelie feelie feelie.

"Let's do this on a regular basis."

"Why not, you're such a nice guy."

Floating on air, tiptoeing from cloud to cloud. I'm in love, I'm in lust, I'm in deep shit. Next day skipping down the corridors of knowledge, pulled, three hard men, the 'RA, boy's version. Shiny Oxfords, bald heads, earrings, short parallels, black socks—the uniform.

"We've been told you're seeing an Orangewoman. Please refrain from this anti-social activity."

"But you don't understand men (men?), feelie, feelie the diddies and the bliff." Smack. Just to clear the wax from my ears.

"Her brother's inside for murder—put your country before your dick or we'll beat the shit out of you."

Silence silence silence lumber lumber lumber feelie feelie feelie. It's all over-flow as the plumber said to his girl.

"Why?"

"I'm frightened."

"Oh."

"Well men how'd I do? The republican cause will never die while I'm alive, sure it won't?"

Blah, blah, blah. School, halcyon days.

"Homework boy, late boy, hair boy, earring boy, cursing boy."

Blackboard compass, whack, whack, whack. The inside of a tractor tyre cut to shape, whack whack, whack. Best years of your life. There was one guy though, history teacher, always talking about Sun Yat-sen and his wee merry men. Community worker, hands across the divide type. Big moustache, no tie, long hair, cord jacket, desert boots—a hip guy. He took a shine to me, used to tell me dirty jokes and let me smoke in the store room. Me and him, him and me. Brought me to the Youth Club, got me interested in table tennis. He used to bring me home when the tartans were on the hunt. Sun Yat-sen and his wee merry men. I'm standing in the gym this night, not half-a-brick's throw away from the table tennis room, watching fellas with low cheek bones beat the shit out of each other. Bang, bang, bang, bang. You see there was a pane of glass missing from one of the windows in the table tennis room and if you had a mind to, if you put yourself out a bit, you could have climbed over the front wall, crawled through the long grass on your elbows and knees like a commando, aimed a gun through the missing pane and [*Pause*] if you had a mind to. A hole in the head, thick purple blood on a cord jacket. A smart man with brains hanging out of him. The ante had just been upped. Men steal lives while boys play games. Skip teak stick ra hey man no prob.

"Let's join up."

"I will if you will."

Ten pence a week—funds. Football teams written in a black book, all code you know. I'm Arsenal, the gunners (ha, ha, ha). No readies forthcoming and it's smack smack smack. Even revolutionaries must think in commercial terms. Education Officer, that's me. Lectures in someone's da's garage that smelt of car oil and home brew. Padraig Pearce, Wolfe Tone, Robert Emmet, Henry Joy McCracken, matinee and evening performances all repeated.

"Who didn't pay their divvies this week? Goody, Goody?"

Stage 1: this is a gun, this is how you clean a gun, this is how you hold a gun, this is how you hide a gun. Stage 2: when being chased while carrying a gun, fall to the ground, roll head over heels or arse over bollocks, stand upright and confront the enemy. Stage

3: scout uniforms and drill. March, march, march, left right, left right, turn left, turn right, attention, at ease, fart, belch, spit, scratch your nuts—all in Irish. Big Day—march down some street in some area to commemorate some guy who was murdered some time ago. Baden Powell gear on, a pair of shades and away we go. Up and down and down and up, up and down and down and up. What a boyo I am, is this worth the price of four singles a week or what. Can yous all see me? Up and down and down and up and away we go. La, la, la, la, la—spotted, informed on, someone out of my da's work. Shout, shout, bawl, bawl, clip round the ear, one less volunteer in the struggle for freedom.

"I want to leave."

"You'll have to get a kicking."

"Don't worry, I'm getting used to it."

Took up Gaelic football after that, a bit of culture in the sporting arena.

"And it's Colm McAlarney over the bar."

Agricultural sports, it's a game for close knit communities who breathe fresh air and there's me alienated and likes the smell of petrol fumes. I was walking down the road one night after training when I was pulled by the 'why don't you go out and catch some terrorists' mob.

"Who are you? Where you coming from? Where you going to? How do you spell your name?"

All the time spread-eagled—normal practice. The boys are full of jungle juice, laughing and joking. Rifle barrel in the middle of my back.

"Why don't you play soccer, you fucker? Republican fucking sport. We know where you live, you bastard."

Still laughing as I ran home. Fuck this for a game of darts, have to get out of here, find myself. The big old U S of A is the place for that. Bring a dram of Irish Whiskey and a piece of linen in case you bump into an old sod for the old sod. I met this thirty stone homosexual drug pusher, ate everything from a bag of coal to a hamburger—just like the movies it was. Heat wave, old folk in

Dallas dropping like flies and there's tomatoes the size of your fist.
Wake up, go to the beach, worship the sun god, get stoned, eat fist-
like tomatoes, get stoned, couple of beers, get stoned, go to bed.
   Bliss.
   "Ireland, never heard of the place."
   "You've a lovely voice, your vocal patterns are so lyrical. It
sounds like you're singing all the time, it's really beautiful."
   "Fuck up and pass the joint."
   "Have a shot, all harps drink whiskey. God bless the ole sod."
Four Green Fields—all crying their lamps out.
   "The British are motherfuckers. Protestants are motherfuckers.
Niggers, yids, pollacks, spicks, wops, chinks, gooks, ruskies and
those no-good low-down bastards who kicked Custer's ass—all
motherfuckers. I'd love to see the place. My granny's from Leeson
Street, did you know that? A civil war, jees, that must be great. Do
you have fish in Ireland?" Eyes opened, mind broadened, time to
go.
   "Say hi to your folks, have a nice journey man."
   I travelled, I broke free, now I'm an enlightened person,
unaffected by my hideous surroundings. I am above the humdrum,
aloft and aloof. Education, back to school, grind grind grind swot
swot swot. University, philosophy, a higher plane. Socrates, Plato,
Aristotle, Heidigger, Sartre, epistemology, phemanonology,
metaphysics, logic. Nationalists-Loyalists, bollocks. Communists,
shoulder to shoulder with your fellow man or woman. Sweat of the
brow, the common good, solicitors digging holes, binmen
performing heart surgery, that's the business. Invited to a meeting
I was, oh aye. Walked into this bar, hole in my jacket to look the
part, full of ole lads society didn't give a toss about and the place
reeked of piss, brilliant.
   "No, I'm afraid we're upstairs."
   A log fire, woolly jumpers, beards and pints of Guinness.
Everyone babbling on about the mating habits of wood pigeons
and obscure French film directors in between giving the capitalist
lackies a verbal pasting.

"When I was younger my history teacher was shot dead. Why do things like that happen?"

"After mating the male sits on the eggs, wood pigeons share their parental responsibilities. Wood pigeons have a lot to teach us if only we would listen."

"Why don't we move downstairs, it's a bit too cosy up here."

"I think we're just fine here—you can enlighten them without mixing with them. God, you're so naive."

And some guy in the corner wearing a 'Save Whale Sperm' t-shirt picks his horses from the *Guardian* and rips a hole in his new denims. On the jukebox they're playing 'Give Peace A Chance'. Give my friggin' head peace. I never went back—not that I was missed, wood pigeons were never my thing.

Then I met a girl, by chance at a dance, not that I ever do, unless I'm drunk and then I can't.

"I love you."

"I love you too."

Ding, dong, ding dong—wedding bells. Went to Spain for our honeymoon, all sun, sand and sangria, just like the brochure said. Met up with this crowd from Belfast.

"It's great to be away."

"Why can't Belfast be like this?"

"I've no problems loving my neighbour."

"Why can't we live together?"

Reaching for my second crate of *San Miguel* and reflecting on the moral decline of the western world I said, "It seems to me or shall I say it is my considered opinion that Communism, on paper at least, is indeed the best system under which humans can live."

"Commie bastard."

You can't win, can you? Holidays out, children in, it's time to settle down. Philosophers don't earn much readies. It's understandable, there's no real need for it in these parts. Then someone says to me, "You look like a tiler." And I thought maybe I do. Mix a bucket of stuff, fire it on the floor, fire it on the wall, get the tiles, slap them on, grout it all up and there you go.

Bathrooms, kitchens, and the odd *en suite*. Life couldn't be better, there's a bit of money coming in, the kids have new uniforms and I'm too old to be chased. I'm thinking this place isn't so bad so long as you stick to a routine (which you can't really help doing 'cause that's the way things are), and ignore everything around you (which is what we all do anyway)—happy days. I even brought the kids down to see the tall ships, I mean to say. It's like you can be here and not really live here—you look but don't see, you hear but don't listen and you think but don't question, it's great. Then my slumber is interrupted. I'm standing in a bathroom this day, slapping on some nearly expensive, wouldn't have them in my own house, pink tiles. Semi-detached, car, caravan, motor bike, two children and a good-looking wife, (I lingered on her for a while, it must be the seven-year itch) who doesn't need to work. This guy worked in Mackies and when things were going bad shifted and earned his crust in Shorts—mobility, good if you can get it. The job's finished, everyone's happy, a cup of tea, put some paper on the sofa before you sit, and some chocolate bickies.

"Will you take a cheque?"

"Certainly, we're here to accommodate you, the customer."

His writing was like my wee lad's and he couldn't spell my name. Now, here's me sometimes working, sometimes not, sometimes money, sometimes potless and there's him flitting from place to place gathering a pile of goodies on the way. Sure it's not his fault, if you've a seat reserved on the gravy train you're hardly going to hang around the station, are you? Why don't I ever cop on? You see whenever I'm pushing the kids round these streets in the Sherman tank, I keep thinking to myself, this is where I've lived all my life, this is my community. But it's not, I don't feel at ease here. My whole life hemmed in, Jesus what a waste.

And now there's a list.

Ends

FREEFALLING
(1996)

Freefalling was first performed at the Ardhowen Theatre, Enniskillen, on 2nd February 1996. The play was directed by Karl Wallace. The cast was as follows:

Her	Anne Bird
Him	Miceal Murphy
Produced	Kabosh/Virtual Reality
Visual Designer	Alison K. Butler
Lighting Design	Susan P
Music	Michael O'Suillehbhaih
Musicians	Scott Herrin, Leslie Herrin
Stage Managers	Angela Walker, John Quinn

[*The stage is clear but for two medium sized tables and two hard backed chairs which will be used by the actors as directed.*]

HIM: Two large fries, a regular coke, cheeseburger without the cheese, banana fritter hold the banana, a bucket of coffee and a monster deluxe, everything in it but the kitchen sink box of culinary delights.

HER: William Pitt the Younger. Will-i-am P-itt the Yo-un-ger. Williampitttheyounger. The Young Pit. Shit pit. Sand pit. Pitbull. He lived, he rattled on about something, he died. Empty head. Empty box. Box the younger. Jesus.

HIM: The guy above me, my boss, the fella that owns my arse, does nothing but give me grief. In his deeper moments he reckons his life's shit so I take the rap for it.

HER [*as* HIS BOSS]: Dirty finger nails, hat not straight and your attitude with the customer is all wrong. Punters are money. Hamburgers are money. Punters, hamburgers, money. Love the punters. Love the hamburgers. Love the money. What does it take to run a good business? What is business? What is the business?

HIM: His wife's giving him gyp 'cause he's never there, he's not getting his end away, the kids drive him mental, the phone bill hasn't been paid and his dog won't stop shitting in the garden— know what I mean?

HER [*as* HIS BOSS]: You look bad, I look bad, the bossman gets on my case. We're a unit. A lean mean fighting machine at the cutting edge of the ever expanding consumer industry. A clean cut fighting unit—it's a war, dog eat dog, man eat dog, dog eat man, man eat hamburger, rip your competitor's fucking throat out. War—win or die?

HIM: Ever hear the like of that, guy sells hamburgers for a living, thinks he's at the fuckin' Alamo. He's in a war zone alright, but that's just life doing that to him, not me. [*To customer*] Sorry luv we don't do kebabs—they're made with real meat. I get his shit it makes him feel good, he gets his boss' shit, his boss feels good—that's the way of it, we all get each other's shit. [*To customer*] Yes sir, it's real lettuce.

HER: Another pencil please. This guy takes me for history—in between mouthing on about all our yesterdays he likes to sneak a wee glance up my skirt.

HIM [*as* LECTURER]: This incitement of the working classes of other countries—very warm isn't it, hot, sticky, sweaty—to revolt was one of the reasons given by Pitt for breaking off relations with France in January 1793—maybe a one-to-one tutorial, more intimate, a deeper understanding of where we're at—the following month France declared war against Britain, and the Revolutionary and Napoleonic wars began.

HER: Nose picking, arse scratching, ear tweeking, ball rubbing type of guy. I give him a good eyeful now and again just to wind him up. In the right frame of mind you could take it as a compliment—he doesn't want to jam his head between the thighs of every student. When I've nothing else to do I think about giving him one just to get rid of him. Slimy Toad.

HIM [*as* LECTURER]: The importance of what I've just said with regard to how we live our lives today is important. It's importance is important. I could even stretch the point and say it's importance is doubly important, that is, beyond the realm of normal importance, moving out to an importance which is itself, by the very fact of its own existence, important—not in the normal sense of the word of course, it's important you understand that.

HER: Important or what? If I could only understand that I'd have it made—just squeeze it in to my jam-packed dome and life would be a tad easier. It won't go in—different positions, different angles—still won't go in. I don't care about it that's why. It doesn't help that his wee blood-shot beady eyes are always fixed on me—it fucks the intellectual ambience up.

HIM: Punters in their droves, day in day out, stuffing their faces tight until you couldn't fit a blade of grass in. Grin from ear to ear, be polite, Sir this and Madam that, and above all else get a shifty. Make like you're happy and shovel the shit out by the tray load. That's the bottom line, as they say. Smiling all the time just pisses people off. People who smile all the time, you want to slap the gob off them. It's like my smile and this hamburger are going to make your dismal, pathetic, futile stretch on this planet honky dorey. I know it won't, they know it won't—that pisses them off. Who am I then? Not the wee lad who serves behind the counter—no, I'm the happy smug bastard who makes people think their lives aren't what they should be—'cause they're not smiling from dawn to dusk—'cause when you do that you haven't a care in the world, have you? [*To customer*] No, you only get a free toy when you buy a mega meal between three and four on a Sunday morning and it's not raining—something to do with the rain making the food disintegrate.

HER: Why am I the only one having a problem with this? Everyone writing nine to the dozen, page after page—one exam and some midget tribe in the Amazon are homeless. Can't remember one damn fact and the knowledge is gushing from the rest of them like they were burst taps. Bookworms. Ask them what time it is they tell you what page they're on. I touched for this guy on my course—wee honey, great ass, nice smile too—everything. Time to have a laugh, let your hair down or at least remove the poker that's jammed firmly up your arse. A few drinks, talk nonsense, kiss and cuddle, see what happens. All I get is, have you handed that essay in, have you read that book, isn't Pitt the shit a fascinating person, where would we be without history? Then when I don't merrily skip into the sack with him he looks shocked, taken aback as if his patter were gold dust I let slip through my fishnets. A threesome, me, him and Willy the Kid—that'd be lovely?

HIM: Wee girl in here I've the hots for, not the best looking in the world, in semi-darkness she has a touch of the Boris Karloff's about her—who am I to talk—she's horny looking that's the thing, that's what rings my bell. The banter between me and her's good—I ask her out in order to let me in. "No," she says, "'cause you're not a boss." She wants to shaft my boss 'cause she thinks that's going to help her in the world. He kicks my ass and she wants to jump on his ass because his kicking my ass turns her ass on. Even in this piss-hole power gets you shafted. She has it sussed—you got to go down to make your way up. I'm no use to her in the 'I'm making my mark on the world stakes'. I'm at the bottom of the shit heap. Not that I imagined at this stage I'd be on a pig's back, I just didn't realise I'd be the boy wiping the pig's arse. [*To customer*] No, sir, we don't do bowls of Irish stew, we don't do bowls of anything. If you want a plastic cup of something that's a different matter—Texan spare ribs, maybe?

HER [*talking to fellow students*]**:** You put that down, I put that down, didn't put that down, put that down, shouldn't have put that down, put that down though, no not that, that—maybe I should've put that down—six questions, an extra one, he told us that did he—other things on my mind—24 pages, two pens and half a pencil—writer's cramp yeah—William Pitt the Younger! I nearly slept with him once—no, not actually—you're right, a silly thing to say, not factual, better to deal in facts—meet up at nine, get blitzed, talk shit, feel superior, touch for an ugly, wake up sick as a pig—great idea, count me in.

HIM [*to customer*]**:** Two fifty seven please. Without the coke? It's still two fifty seven, the coke's free. It's only free when you buy the meal. You're right it's not free, you pay for it through the nose. It's all a rip off is it? You don't want it now, right. The smiling pisses you off does it, you'd like to kick my fuck in but you won't because you're a Christian. Yeah I'll do that, I'll thank God later. Two chicken sandwiches and a portion of barbecue

beans and black coffee. Make that a large portion, no chicken
sandwiches and kiwi fruit milkshake. It's going to be the same
rigmarole tonight—same every week. Meet up with a few
mates, sink a couple of pints, bitch in each other's face about
how work's a real pisser, strut your stuff in front of the women,
talk about their tits, wee, big, sticky up, droopy down, taunt
each other about who we're going to bang, how often we've
banged, how great we are at banging, sink a few more pints, talk
balls about football, grab the ugliest woman in Christendom,
put it to her, get knocked back, get pissed, buy a Chinese, spill
half, throw half up, in to bed with the clothes on, try and have
a wank, fail, sleep and wake up with a tongue like a baboon's
arse. Happy days. [*To customer*] Sorry luv, my shift's over, I'm
out of here.

[*They both walk on the spot.*]

HER: The gardens where I live are treated like people, groomed,
cared for, talked to, talked about, they have an identify of their
own—like an addition to the family, it's a wonder they're not
given names.

HIM: Bloody dog shit. Woof, woof. Fuck off.

HER: People up here talk to their gardens but not each other,
except when they're throwing barbecues, then they sip, chew,
suck, gulp, never puke, kiss each other on the cheek then knife
each other in the back—about their gardens. Semi-detached,
leafy suburbia—lego land.

HIM: They bring their dogs from streets away to shit in our street.
Dogs chasing cars in wee terraced streets. Woof, woof, woof.
Fuck off.

HER: A couple moved in next door, he's an architect, she's a civil
servant. Two blonde children always dressed like they're just
about to get their photographs taken. Say cheese. He's a suit
and she's draped in the latest from Marks & Sparks. The
garden's a picture, the house straight out of Habitat. There's
a saloon car in the drive shining like a diamond. Whenever he's
not drawing pictures of boxes, he's fixing things, Mr. DIY,

pressed overalls, checked shirt and every tool known to man hanging from his skinny hips. Whenever she's not filling out forms and making life shit for people who's lives already are shit, she's teaching little Ken and Barbie good manners and cooking dinner which she froze the night before in between plucking unwanted hair from her nipples and giving herself a good hosedown with a strawberry flavoured douche to get rid of the grime. My parents love them, you can see it in their cheesey grins, it's what they want for me, not that they'd ever say that, it's not in their nature. The ones next door, I hate them. They're nice people, that's why I hate them. They hold their niceness up like a trophy for the rest of the world to admire. Fuck that.

HIM: Tall houses, plenty of rooms, kids, tiny concrete gardens— where the kids can't play.

"Hear about her in 53."

"No."

"Had a man in."

"No."

"Big argument—the shouts and screams of her."

"No."

"I phoned the peelers."

"She's never been right in the head since her man died."

"I know."

"Riff raff."

"I know."

You can't take a leek in the sink here without it going to press. Live out of each other's pockets and there's something wrong with you if you don't marry the girl two streets away. The guy facing us, a binman, married the girl next door. His brother, also a binman, married his brother's wife's cousin and live four doors away. Their sister, who's married to a guy who wants to be a binman lives in the next street. The other sister who's not married, there's talk about her being a lesbian, lives two streets away in the same house as the ma does, although they haven't talked in five years after one of them blew the grocery money on the bingo. They all have three or four kids, except for the lesbian, and they all use the ma's house to sit and bitch about each other. Which the ma loves because she's getting on in years and has nothing else to do but bingo herself and sit and talk about other people. My ma and da think that's normal—fuck that caper for a game of darts.

HER: Your life's mapped out. To them it's a good job well done if they find me a place in the world. The only place they know is their own, so that's the direction they go. Like the University thing, it was something just assumed. My opinion on that— diddly-squat. Worked for us so it'll work for you. That might be alright but it doesn't stop there—no, now they have expectations. Some squinty-eyed little dullard is trying to grab a glimpse of my fanny and they have expectations. Responsibility you see—they have it, it's a burden to them, it defines their lives, so now they want me to have a piece of it so it can define my life. And it's not like you can tell them stuff like that—they think they're open—well actually they are, but it's their holes not their minds.

HIM: Talk, talk, talk all the time—yap, yap, yap, rabbit, rabbit, rabbit—but nobody says anything, nothing that matters anyway. Like the grief I'm getting at work, you can't bring that gear into the house—it's a rule no grief from the outside world allowed in through the front door—no room for it that's why, plenty of grief here already. Make no odds anyway, my da'd be the exact same as the shithead who's giving me the problems—he's from the 'you got to learn the hard way' school of philosophy. That's the way it was for him so if it's that way for me he's happy as a pig in shit—which he is.

HIM/HER: I'm home.

HIM [*as* HER PARENTS]: "Education's the most important thing in the world my girl. Isn't that right, father?"

"Correct mother—that and your golf handicap."

"It's the solid, righteous, educated men and women of the

world that are the ... what are they father?"

"The educated, solid and righteous, that's what they are."

"That's right father. What your father and I have given up to put you through the education system, it's—what is it father?"

"A disgrace. We deprived ourselves of things no straight thinking people should deprive themselves of. Right or wrong Mother?"

"Correct."

"Tell her the deprivation stories, mother."

"Sorry, I was just thinking those curtains would look better back to front, good side out."

"Excellent, but the deprivation stories, dear."

"I remember days when your father had clients round and we had no cocktail sticks for the sliced bananas because I had just purchased writing sticks for you. That right father?"

"No cocktail sticks, no banana slices—disaster."

"But you're a good girl, you'll do the right thing, won't she do the right thing father?"

"Do the right thing."

HER [*as* HIS PARENTS]: "Your rooms like a pig sty—isn't it like apigsty missus?"

"Like a pig sty mister—a shit-hole of a pig sty that only a filthy, dirty, lazy, useless, scumbag, fuck hawk, wipe your arse on the curtains type of fucker would live in."

"Well put, missus."

"Thank you, mister."

"Hard work, hard work means keeping your room ship shape. Ship shape, missus."

"Ship shape, mister—not like this dirty fucking, whore's melt, fucking—"

"Enough's enough, missus."

"Sorry, mister."

"You get nothing for nothing in this world. Nothing for nothing, something for something, nothing for something and something for nothing. Something for nothing, missus."

"Something for something, mister."

"Don't contradict me, you dopey bitch."

"No contradictions here, mister."

"Work hard, knuckle down and you'll always have a tenner in your pocket. Always a tenner in the pocket, missus."

"Give us it."

"Fuck off."

HIM/HER: I'm away out.

[*Walking on the spot*]

HIM: Smells.

HER: Noises.

HIM: Hustle.

HER: Bustle.

HIM: Combing.

HER: Roaming.

HIM/HER: The city lights.

HIM: Awake to

HER: And awash with

HIM/HER: Everything a discerning individual like myself could ever wish for.

HER [*as a* DRUNK MAN]: Alright son—getting there—what—a few shillings—a smoke—fuck ye—bastards—fuck the lot of them—fuck all about fuck all—that right son?

HIM [*as a* BIBLE THUMPER]: Ye who is not born again shall suffer darkness and damnation for all eternity.

HER [*as* DRUNK MAN]: Jesus Christ.

HIM [*as a* BIBLE THUMPER]: Suffering is our saviour—without the Lord's forgiveness we are thrown without mercy into the fires of hell.

HER [*as* DRUNK MAN]: Fuck all fornicators—right kid—any big sisters?

HIM [*as* BUSKER]: "Come gather round people wherever you roam and admit that the waters around you have grown."

HER [*as* ROWDY YOUTHS]: Here we go, here we go, here we go—want my cough rock huh—get that right up your bangle—what—

huh?

HIM [*as* BUSKER]: "Well I'm a one man band nobody knows nor understands."

HER [*as* DRUNK MAN]: Fuck 'em bastards—me—me I'm alright—I know the fuckin' crack—bastards.

HIM [*as a* BIBLE THUMPER]: "There are ways which seem right unto a man, but the end thereof are the ways of death."

HER [*as* ROWDY YOUTHS]: You want that in ye or what? Fuckin' lesbian you are—sort you out, cure ye of that. Here we go, here we go.

HER [*as* BOUNCER *to* HIM]: Two pound in, any acrobatin', I sort you out, straight out on your arse.

HIM [*as* BOUNCER *to* HER]: Away you on in luv—come the death you still on your lonesome I'll see what I can do for you.

[*They enter a crowded bar.*]

HER: Excuse me.

HIM: Sorry.

HER: Can I get by there?

HIM: Excuse me.

HER: Pint of cider.

HIM: Bottle of beer.

HER: Excuse me.

HIM: Sorry.

HER: Can I get by there?

HIM: Excuse me.

[*Centre stage—talking to strangers*]

HER: You think poetry is more important than food then?

HIM: Breast implants—the size of two small melons, there you go.

HER: Rather starve to death than remain unknown and that would be a Catch 22 because starving would make you known.

HIM: But she was too near the fire was she—melted?—mountains to fried eggs?—dear God.

HIM/HER: Sorry there are other people—yeah—do that—there just over there—will do—if I could just get—yes certainly will.

[*Walking backwards to opposite sides of the stage.*]

HER: I'll look forward to reading it—underground press—of

course yes.

HIM: Send me pictures after the operation—you too—thank you for sharing with me.

HIM/HER: Jesus.

[*Sit at tables. Among friends. Replying to conversations.*]

HER: I already have a drink—I don't want to get blocked—I'm not stopping any of the rest of yous am I? I just don't want to—leave it just do what you have to do.

HIM: Right we all have shit jobs and what—that's my point, bitching about the shit jobs only makes the evening shit—it's not the only thing in our lives.

HER: All I'm saying is going to university isn't always the best thing in the world—people who don't go are missing something out is that it? Superior? That's a lot of bloody nonsense.

HIM: I can see her, yes she's lovely big diddies—you haven't touched for three months that's why—stop saying that, either go over and put it to her and get it out of your system or forget about it—no you ask her.

HER: No you go over and ask him—he's a geek—picky? I'm picky because I don't want some geek with his tongue down my throat and his grubby hands up my jumper.

HIM: It's only a game how can it depress you—cried when they hit the bar get a grip—you met any of them no—they don't give a shit about you so why should you give a twopenny fig about them.

[*Moving towards centre stage*]

HER: William Pitt?

HIM: Banged her three times?

HER: Blow job in the taxi?

HIM: Massive diddies?

HER: Law exams?

HIM: Cup final?

HIM/HER: [*Shout*] Enough.

[*Back in the* street]

HER [*as* DRUNK MAN]: Alright kid—few extra shillings.

HIM: What? What is it you want? [*Emptying pockets*] Money, fags, what?

HER [*as* DRUNK MAN]: A few shillings, son?

HIM: Take the lot, here take the keys of the house if you're stuck for somewhere to kip there's a bed there. Jump in with my ma if you want, my da'll be on the sofa anyway. Take the lot everything.

HER [*as* DRUNK MAN]: Think I'm a dickhead aye—fuck you.

HIM: Fuck you. [*As* BIBLE THUMPER] The Lord welcomes sinners into his arms. [*She makes masturbatory gestures.*] The Lord punishes those who worship at the altar of sin.

HER: Go to hell.

[*Both walking on the spot.*]

HIM: That's what I look forward to after knocking my pan in week in, week out. Jesus. It's that type of thing that kills people— slowly, very slowly it wipes the smile from their faces, the same life over and over again. Like, we're all caught in a revolving door. You go in thinking you're going to get out the other side but it just keeps going round and round. You get confused, exhausted, loose your sense of direction and it just keeps going round and round. Then suddenly it just throws you out but you're not at the other side, you're just back where you started, standing there watching the others go round and round and wishing you were there even though you know it's pointless because it's all you've got. But it's too late you can't get back in, the war's over. Back there in the bar that was the beginning of my revolving door journey. Time to get off I think.

HER: What was all that about? What was going on back there? Huddled together round a table, might as well have been a million miles apart. It's all look at me, listen to me, I'm important, I've important things to say, masked by the pretentious friendly banter of course. Egos ricocheting off each other but nothing ever lands, nothing ever caught—no contact, like we were all talking to each other through oxygen tents. No bond, nothing to hold on to except the lie, that we're all, by choice, deep, acutely aware and sensitive soul mates. If I fail they'll all be glad, they'd say the opposite of course but I know different. Success is all the sweeter when someone else falters at the finishing line. That's the way they'll always be too. And people see me with them and think I'm one of them—a clone tarred with the same brush. I don't think so.

HIM/HER: There's more to life than slowly slipping unnoticed into the grey zone. Where's the bite, the kick, that moment when you stand alone, reaching out to grab what's yours. A time to step outside the drab, dreary, humdrum and wave bye-bye. A time to let yourself go.

[*They sit at opposite ends of a park bench.*]

HER: Bored?

HIM: Shitless.

HER: The park's lovely in the evening—tranquil.

HIM: What?

HER: Tranquil—the park.

HIM: Yeah. Do you sit here a lot?

HER: First time.

HIM: Me too.

HER: Kismet.

HIM: Bless you. My name's—

HER: No—no names. Two people on a park bench that's all.

HIM: No names!

HER: And no details.

HIM: Mystery, I like that.

HER: Basking in life's sweet mystery.

HIM: You're not going to give it all this heavy shit are you?

HER: Heavy shit. Me? No.

HIM: Good. Heavy shit always tends to put a dampner on the mood I think.

HER: What mood?

HIM: Two strangers on a park bench just saying stuff type of mood.

HER: Saying anything we want?

HIM: Anything you want.

HER: Just let go.

HIM: Two strangers just letting go.

HER: Alright. Where are we then?

HIM: On a park bench.

HER: Come on, anything you said—just let yourself go.

HIM: A beach in Spain.

HER: No, a beach in Spain's no good, too ordinary.

HIM: The moon, we're on the moon.

HER: That it? I've a choice between some poxy beach in Spain and the moon.

HIM: I didn't say it was poxy, it was going to be a beautiful beach, a beautiful empty beach.

HER: Given a free hand it's a bit limited isn't it, not very creative or exciting—where's the violence, the sex, the thrill, all that stuff.

HIM: I was only starting, we could've screwed a couple of Martians then wiped them out.

HER: Aye.

HIM: Alright you go, you start, seeing you're not too keen on screwing and killing aliens—not creative enough. Welt away there.

HER: Touchy.

HIM: Bullshit, just start.

HER: All I meant was it didn't seem much of a fantasy—that's all.

HIM: What fantasy? Who mentioned fantasy? You, me, who?

HER: I thought that's what we were talking about—anything you want, just let yourself go you said.

HIM: Right, right I got it. I'm Jim Morrison of The Doors getting a blow job in a lift.

HER: You can't be someone else, it has to be you.

HIM: It would be me, I'd be Jim Morrison.

HER: No. Look , you can be a rock star getting a blow job in a lift but you can't be Jim Morrison.

HIM: There's rules now? Fantasies with rules? The whole point is there is no rules, let your napper drift into the wild blue yonder.

HER: You're a rock star getting a blow job in a lift and what?

HIM: And nothing, that's it, that's my fantasy.

HER: Who's giving you the blow job?

HIM: I don't know, some woman.

HER: Who, a stranger, a groupie, your granny, who?

HIM: Your granny—something wrong with your head? Who's going to have a fantasy like that—yuk—your granny and that other gear, I don't even like saying it. It's sick.

HER: It can be sick.

HIM: You're sick—if we're starting all that shit count me out. Your granny, not even your auntie where there's a vague possibility but your fucking granny.

HER: Something real but not real, something that might happen but won't—got it.

HIM: I'll start again.

HER: Good idea.

HIM: I'm still a rock star.

HER: Thought you might be.

HIM: Open air concert, twenty thousand—no half a million screaming fans, hands above heads, clapping in unison. I'm back stage, they're waiting on me. The noise is deafening, like your eardrums are going to burst right open. I turn round and behind me there's a lift, I see my granny walk into it, I think fuck that. *Eddie, Eddie*—that's not my real name by the way. *Eddie, Eddie.* Reporters, cameras—click, click, flash, flash. Bodyguards clearing a path. Questions shouted at me. "People are saying you're Satan's son, Eddie, are you?" "Are you as mad as they say?" I spit in the reporter's face and smack another one round the head with a guitar. Laughing. "Crazy that, fuck face." I grab some chick, ram my tongue down her throat then hit her a slap, she loves it. *Eddie, Eddie, Eddie.* Noise deafening. Lights blinding. Fuck the shit-hole I grew up in this is where I'm meant to be. [*Stands up on bench.*] On stage. I am a god. *Eddie, Eddie, Eddie.* The blood pumping through my veins, the crowd chanting, the blood pumping, heart bursting. I'm on fire, red hot blood surging through every sinew. "I'm back"—the crowd—*yeah.*

"Fuck you—do you hear me—fuck you." A thick, solid, heaving mass screaming "Fuck you, fuck you, fuck you." "Do you want me?" *Yeah.* "Can't hear it." *Yeah.* My guitar blows them away like a noise, a sound they've never heard before—electrifying. Power. Unity. Purity. Dive from the stage into the sweaty heap. Hands groping, grabbing, pulling. Open mouths screaming, yelping, squealing—they all want a piece, their lives will be complete if they can only touch the King. I'm going under then they surge forward and lift me up presenting me to the heavens like the Messiah. A helicopter in the sky. A rope ladder dangles. Still playing I piss on the crowd below. *Eddie, Eddie, Eddie.* Away, flying way, the King has gone.

HER: Where?

HIM: What?

HER: Where? Where does the King go? You're a hero, be hero like.

HIM: I'm in the chopper, my girl's stoned. I get stoned and we fuck the shit out of each other. Flying just flying—open space and flight. Flying.

HER: Where? Flying where?

HIM: The best rock musician that every walked the face of this earth. Award ceremony, we're flying to an award ceremony. Chopper lands on the top of a hotel roof—blades come to a halt. We're late—panic. Fuck the ceremony. She has a bottle of Jack Daniels, we sit on the roof sucking the bottle. High above the city at night. High up—soft sounds, blurred lights, the hum of movement—beautiful. Looking out over the world misunderstood and looking out over the world. "Can you fly baby doll? Can you fly?"

HER: I can fly.

HIM: "Fly with me, let's soar above like free birds in the breeze." We jump—a moment, the only moment—alive—free—floating— we smile and kiss. *Eddie, Eddie, Eddie.* Bang, splat, dead.

HER: *Eddie, Eddie, Eddie.*

HIM [*playing the guitar*]: Go for it baby, straight into it—go.

HER: I'm ripping up the road on a Harley Davison, nothing but open road and shiny chrome. I've a pair of shades on, a black evening dress and a leather biker jacket. Burning rubber in the hot summer heat. I'm free, I'm alone and I'm going to do some damage. The winds in my hair and I know no fear—I'm invincible. Ever watch the movie *Taxi Driver* with de Niro in it?

HIM: You can't be de Niro—Jim Morrison was tossed aside, the same goes for de Niro.

HER: A black evening dress?

HIM: Sorry. Right.

HER: *Taxi Driver*? The movie?

HIM: Aye saw it, good show—like your wee woman playing the brass nail, she was good.

HER: Remember de Niro in front of the mirror—"You talking to me? Are you talking to me? You fucking talking to me?" That's the feeling I have, complete control. The heat would crack a stone, I'm parched and there's beads of sweat trickling down my back. Pull over at a garage, nothing around for miles but empty open fields. Standing drinking a cold bottle of beer, rubbing the bottle against my face, licking the ice cold glass. "You want some gas?"

HIM: Gas?

HER: I'm in America.

HIM: Right, got ye.

HER: "You want some gas?" He's nothing special—but a good body and a nice smile, perfect pearly whites. He's nervous—I'm making him nervous—a young, fresh, shaky little boy. I take him by the hand and lead him into the toilets. A delicate peck on the check—then I screw him til his eyes pop out of their sockets. A moment he'll remember for the rest of his poxy, boring little life. He's spoiled—I spoiled him. He's broken—I broke him. Another delicate little peck on the cheek and I'm gone—back burning rubber in the blistering heat. I'm going to do something bad—I'm a bad girl. Today's a bad day for someone. The bike's cruising, I'm cruising—the heat seeping into my face—the power between my thighs the gentle vibrations of the bike are making my teeth itch—I can taste the salty sweat on my lips. I need another cold beer. Some shit covered, Hicksville, out in the arsehole of nowhere, redneck, little place. I stroll in—tall, lean, straight. I slip the jacket off. "Hello boys." Fat little beady eyes, sweaty smelly bodies—toothless grins. They're thinking, here's some fun, a little girl on her own—manna from heaven, The Lord's Prayer answered.

"You lost your way, little missy?"

"Looking for some company, little missy?"

"We're all friendly boys round these parts."

"You fuck many sheep round these parts boys—you look like a lot of sheep fuckers to me—am I right or am I right?" The boys aren't impressed.

"That's bad talk for a little missy—we might have to teach you a lesson, right boys—some good old down-to-earth manners."

"Fuck you."

"That's trouble, little missy."

"I'm trouble, motherfucker."

I grab the barman by the hair and smack his head against the counter, then I produce the bad news—one shot blows his head fucking clean off. Thick purple blood dripping from the counter—drip, drip, drip. "Want to play boys—headless fucking chickens." Panic, running for cover but there's nowhere to hide. My hands covered in blood I suck one of my fingers. "Finger licking good boys." Bang, bang, bang. Wasted. The hero, the talker, the big man, the leader of the pack—I save him for last. "Have a seat, rest yourself, your look tired." The blood's left his face, he's wet his trousers, he wants to speak but he can't—just mumbling. "You're mumbling." I rest the gun against his temple, then stroke his face. He's gasping for air. "Look me in eye boy—that's better. Just not your day is it, or maybe it is." Fuck it, let's steal a car. Do you hear me?

HIM: Who're you talking to?

HER: You. A car—we'll steal a car.

HIM: You out of your mind, steal a car—what for?

HER: A laugh, have some real thrills—just to do something crazy.

HIM: Aye sure.

HER: It'll be alright, just steal a car drive it around for a while then bring it back.

HIM: You serious?

HER: Yeah, do something different, have a laugh.

HIM: I'm not stealing any car—fuck that. You can have all the crazy shit of the day floating about in your napper—fine—stealing cars is something else, there's consequences to that, you're messing with other people's stuff, you understand. Does the word 'caught' mean anything to you?

HER: We'll not get caught, we're only taking it for a spin, where's the harm in that—it'll be a laugh. Haven't you ever wanted to break out, do something you don't normally do—that's all it is. We're not going to keep it, we'll leave it back—have a thrill, pump yourself up, that's all.

HIM: Can we not just steal a bottle of milk from someone's doorstep, or stay out all night drinking with winos under a bridge or something? Jesus, stealing a car.

HER: If there's no danger there's no thrill. When your fifty and wishing you had someone else's life because yours is shit it'll be something to look back on—the night you did something different—the moment you walked on the wild side—the day you told the world to stick it up its arse—come on.

HIM: Shit.

HER: What?

HIM: Alright, alright we'll do it. Shit.

HER: What?

HIM: I just realised I'm going to steal a car, it panics me you know, so the word 'shit' keeps popping out. Shit.

HER: The thrills working already, the blood's pumping, the heart's pounding—we're alive.

HIM: Shit. Right we have to think about this.

HER: Can you drive?

HIM: Aye. Can you not?

HER: No.

HIM: Excellent, great, hunky-fucking-dory—so it's me stealing the car now.

HER: We'll both be in it, what difference does it make who's driving it? A nice black one, I think that's what we should go for.

HIM: A black one—a nice black one?

HER: Yeah, black cars look sexy.

HIM: I'm no expert on this but I'm certain that when stealing a car colour isn't very important—the easiest type to break in to, the one nearest you or hope upon hope, one with keys in it—colour no.

HER: It's just it would feel all wrong if we stole a crappy one, wouldn't it—if we're going to do it, do it in style.

HIM: The seedy underworld's going to welcome us with open arms aren't they—whenever we apply for our gangster membership cards we'll tell them we specialise in stealing sexy cars so we can look good.

HER: If we're caught isn't it better to look the part.

HIM: After we steal it we'll work out what outfits we're going to wear so we don't clash—that's typical women shit that.

HER: Oh, don't be a dick.

HIM: Another thing stop using the word 'caught', it's not a useful word at the moment.

HER: Sorry, I'm sure.

HIM: Aye. There's one over there—that's it.

HER: It's green.

HIM: We're eco hoods, if anyone asks tell them we're on a mission to save the fuckin' ozone. The window's open.

[*They make their way cautiously to where the car is.*]

HIM: If the alarm goes off run like fuck.

HER: Where to?

HIM: You're determined to make life difficult for me aren't you?

HER: I'm only asking—I'm new to this—it's not like I instinctively know what to do.

HIM: Do I look like a car thief?

HER: You do a bit yeah.

HIM: What does that mean—a fucking car thief?

HER: If your face was to pop up on TV and they said you were a car thief you wouldn't look out of place that's all.

HIM: Do I look like a car thief?

HER: I'm sorry I said it now.

HIM: Tell me—it would be a handy thing to know in case I'm ever going for a job in a garage or something—have to wear some type of disguise wouldn't I? Tell me.

HER: You just have that look about you that you might do something wrong, not stealing a car—anything. That's all, that's all I meant.

HIM: That's all, you tell me I look like a fucking criminal and that's it.

HER: It's not like I said you were ugly—you just have a look about you—Jesus.

HIM: Thank God, I'd hate to look like one of the Kray Twins and be ugly.

HER: I was wrong—you look like Francis of Assisi—you look like butter wouldn't melt in your mouth.

HIM: Look like a fucking criminal. It's open—get in.

[*In the car*]

HER: Right.

HIM: Right what?

HER: Start it or will we just sit here and made car noises.

HIM: I'm thinking alright—thinking. Give me one of your shoes.

HER: What for?

HIM: I like driving in women's shoes—to break open the fucking steering thing, just give me it.

HER: Don't break the heel.

HIM: Look like a fucking criminal.

HER: You connect the wires together, you just twist them round or something—you see it all the time in the movies.

HIM: I'm doing that. Can't you see that I'm doing that.

HER: I'm only trying to help.

HIM: You're not—I don't know what I'm doing here—just keep quiet.

HER: Can I have my shoe back?

HIM: On the floor.

HER: Shit, is someone coming?

HIM: The shoe's on the fucking floor.

[*She bends down. He gets the car started.*]

HIM: Jesus, it's started—class—I got it to start—move til I get at the gear stick.

HER: I'm stuck, my jumper's caught.

HIM: Fuck. Fuck. Move.

HER: I'm fucking trying—shut up. Shit it's ripping it.

HIM: You're fucking ripping it. Right, right, right—calm down. Pull the jumper slowly up and move back.

[*She gets free. They sit in silence and smile.*]

HER: Burn rubber.

HIM: Burn rubber.

[*Driving music. Music down. She stands arms in air.*]

HER: Let the forces of the universe be with us. Let the wind rip through your bones. The earth below and the heavens above, we are the masters of all before us. The beauty of the night. We are free—let us be born again.

HIM: You tell them kid—sing it out there baby.

HER: Fuck the world.

HIM: Fuck it.

HER: Make my day assholes.

HIM: Make it assholes.

HER: Let the boring ones suck dirt.

HIM: Dirt—suck—boring

HER: We shall fly like eagles and shit on the drowning heap below.

HIM: Eagles—shit—heap—drowning.

HER: Up, up and away to the moon, I can jump off the moon. I am a God.

HIM: Off the moon—God.

HER: Kiss my rectum.

[*He does. Laughter.*]

HER: Pull over, pull over there's a wee pub up ahead, we'll have a drink. I need a drink.

HIM: No, we're going back. A wee spin and a few laughs—we've done it—time to go back—get offside—happy days.

HER: Please, please, please, please, please.

HIM: No, we do that we're looking for trouble—the car parked outside the place, somebody spots it then what? No.

HER: Just to finish the whole thing off—two tearaways on the run—walking on the wild side, stroll in like two gangsters—de Niro "You talking to me. You fucking talking to me." Come on, one drink, have a laugh, mess the locals about—come on.

HIM: One drink.

HER: Yes—after one we'll head back.

HIM: Promise.

HER: Cross my heart and hope to die. "You talking to me? You fucking talking to me?"

[*Move from car to bar. Laughter. Jovial play acting. Walking like gangsters.*]

HER: We're here. Hello boys, slap my thighs and kick the shit off my boots.

[*A dance sequence indicating they are beaten up. Thrown out, they crawl back into the car.*]

HER: Start the fucking car—start the car.

HIM: Shit, I think my hand's broken—Christ—shit.

HER: Bastards—dirty bastards.

HIM: You're going to have to work the gears—shit my hand.

HER: I can't drive.

HIM: Just do it.

HER: I can't drive.

HIM: Shut the fuck up and do what I tell you.

HER: A hanky—there's blood in my eye, I need a hanky.

HIM: I don't know—fuck—hanky—fuck—in there, any fucking where.

HER: Look.

HIM: The gears, look at the fucking gears—shit.

HER: Look—a gun.

HIM: Jesus—fuck—shit. Jesus. Put it back. No get rid of it, throw it out the window.

HER: A gun.

HIM: Out—the gun out.

HER: No.

HIM: What?

HER: No—I'm just going to scare them.

HIM: Fuck them—you're scaring me.

HER: Calm down—just scare them that's all—wave it about, point it at them, put the shit up them that's all. Fuck them.

HIM: It's a gun.

HER: Fuck them, a bit of fear in their heads—fuck them. I'm doing it. You coming with me?

HIM: No. Yes. No. Yes. I don't know what I'm doing.

HER: Put the shit up the bastards. Keep the car running. You coming with me?

HIM: Yes. Yes.

[*Move from car to bar*]

HER: Remember us. [*Pointing gun*] Do you remember who the fuck we are? Now it's our turn for the fucking fun.

HIM [*as* CUSTOMER]: Just put the gun away like a good little girl.

HER: Don't move.

HIM [*as* CUSTOMER. *Moving towards her*]: Little girls who play with things they shouldn't sometimes get punished—you don't want that.

HER: Don't fucking move I said—you fucker don't move.

HIM [*as* CUSTOMER. *Lifts a stick*]: I don't think you're going to use that—you're a sweet little girl.

HER [*screams*]: Fuck.

[*She shoots. He falls to the ground. She shoots the other occupants of the bar. They stand in silence. Run to car. Driving music. Music down. Car stops. He falls out onto his hands and knees and vomits.*]

HER: Are you alright?

HIM: Get to fuck away from me—don't touch me—don't come near me.

HER: I'm sorry.

HIM: Sorry.

HER: It's the only thing I can think of to say—I'm sorry.

HIM: Fuck. I need to think. Fuck.

HER: I'm sorry.

HIM: Shut up, stop fucking saying it—it means nothing, fuck all, zero, nothing.

HER [*cries*]: Stop shouting at me.

HIM: Shouting at you—stop fucking shouting at you—what I'm being over-insensitive am I? Sorry about that, it's just my whole life has been fucked up—it makes me a bit touchy, a bit edgy you know.

HER: I'm sorry.

HIM: Zero. Nothing. Fuck all. Meaningless. Let's steal a car, it'll be a bit of fun. Let's call in somewhere and mess the punters about it's only a laugh. Oh look, we have shooter now let's scare them a bit, oh no sorry I've changed my mind let's blow them all off the face of the earth—sure if you're going to have a laugh you might as well go for the fucking big one.

HER: He was going—

HIM: Fuck up—don't talk just fuck up. No do talk, pour your guts out, spew your thoughts up—let's hear it—what? Don't be silent, now's not a time to be fucking silent you understand. Speak.

HER: He was going to do us real damage, you saw him, he was going to hurt both of us.

HIM: Him. One. Uno. Singular. You lived it out didn't you? You fucking lived it out. What's it really like? That's it isn't it—what's it really like?

HER: I ...

HIM: What?

HER: I ...

HIM: What—fucking say it.

HER: I just did it, that's all. I just did it. It's like it wasn't me and they weren't them—not like a real thing—not like something that happens. He frightened me—he really frightened me.

HIM: You get a kick out of it—heart pounding, blood pumping through the veins—watching them, one by one, like ducks at a kids' pop gun stall—I'm here—bang—I'm gone—you got a kick—you win your cuddly toy, did you. Feel good did it?

HER: Yeah, it felt like I was in control—I had all the time in the world and it was my time—I was in control. I had power—"You talking to me? You fucking talking to me?"

HIM: You're meant to keep that shit inside your head—the bad stuff floating about your napper is there to help you get through the day, help you escape for a moment—if fantasy's came true you have fuck all left, it's over, finished.

HER: I didn't want it to happen.

HIM: How do I know that—all seemed to fit into place very fucking easily didn't it—one minute it's a lot of words, next it's the big picture—how do I know what to think?

HER: I just wanted to frighten them that's all—then he frightened me, he frightened me too much. Anybody would've done the same.

HIM: Not me—I know that for sure—not me.

HER: You different from the rest of us.

HIM: No, you are—the rest of us don't wipe people out because we feel we're trapped in a corner. All we had to do was drive off, that's what I would've done, put the kicking down to experience and just drove off.

HER: Why didn't you?

HIM: What?

HER: Why didn't you drive off? I can't drive, there was nothing I could do about it, all you had to do was drive off—why didn't you drive off?

HIM: You wanted to go in, isn't that what you said, isn't that what you wanted to do, you wanted to go in.

HER: Fuck me, I'm nothing to you, why didn't you do what you wanted—what any normal person would've done—why didn't you drive off?

HIM: You rushed me. I couldn't think straight, you put pressure on me, I couldn't think straight.

HER: You were there because you wanted to be there.

HIM: Bollicks.

HER: You were angry, you wanted those fuckers sorted out. All you had to do was watch. Normal person. They got what they deserved, fuck them, that's what you were thinking. You got what you wanted without having to do the dirty work yourself— no blood on your hands. Like one of the titillated crowd watching the hangman go about his business. He's doing the right thing, it has to be done but don't ask me to soil my hands, I'm a moral, righteous, upstanding citizen—a normal person, who once they've watched the dirty deed, go home and bath the kids knowing the world's a safer place.

HIM: Not with psychos like you in it.

HER: You think so? Maybe you're right, maybe it was there all the time. [*Points the gun at him*] Maybe you're next on the list. What do you think? Are you next on the list? I'll get to know what's inside your head by blowing it wide open will I? [*Gun against temple*] This is what I do is it—is it?

[*He grabs the gun from her. Pulls her to the floor and puts gun to her face.*]

HIM: Fuck you, fuck you. You like that do you? Big fucking turn on is it, huh? Where? In the head? The face, the pretty face? What about down here—huh—that would be a bigger turn on wouldn't it—blow the cunt away—right up inside—bang—the ultimate fuck.

HER: Come on normal guy you can do it.

HIM: Bitch.

HER: Discover something about yourself normal guy? It's only a second away isn't it—tick, tock, tick, tock.

[*He drops the gun and hits her with his fist.*]

HER: That feel good did it—get a kick—where you pumping?

[*He hits her again.*]

HER: Feel good normal guy.

[*He lifts his hand to hit her again. Stops. Silence. They kiss. Lights dim then come up again. The two are huddled together under a coat.*]

HER: I'm freezing.

HIM: Pull the coat up over ye.

HER: I'm still cold—let's go back to the car.

HIM: No, we're better off here.

HER: We'll light a fire.

HIM: What with?

HER: Twigs, bits of wood, leaves—whatever there is.

HIM: We've nothing to light it with.

HER: You rub two pieces of wood together very quickly then you blow gently on the spark—you see it on nature programmes all the time, guys with beards rub bits of sticks together, next thing they're cooking dead animals.

HIM: I saw a programme where the guy used the resin from trees to make candles with.

HER: Right we'll do that then.

HIM: He was in the jungle, it was the resin of rubber trees or something.

HER: We'll rub the sticks together then, look I'm going to freeze to death here.

HIM: Rub sticks together, who am I, Robinson Crusoe—I live in the city—we want heat we put a shovel of coal on the fire—in the street where I live we've moved on from the caveman stuff—we can't have a fire anyway—somebody might see the smoke, we don't want to be drawin' attention to ourselves.

HER: I'm still cold.

HIM: Move closer, get some body heat.

HER: Shift your legs over—that's better.

HIM: Do I not get any of the coat now?

HER: That better?

HIM: Yes.

HER: Comfy?

HIM: I'm cold, wet, starvin', frightened and in the middle of a fuckin' forest, how could I be comfy?

HER: Under the circumstances.

HIM: Under the circumstances, yes.

HER: Good.

[*Silence*]

HIM: What was that?

HER: What?

HIM: That noise.

HER: I didn't hear anything.

HIM: It was like a scream or something—yeah a scream or something like that.

HER: We're in the country, there's animals roaming about isn't there.

HIM: What animals roaming about?

HER: I don't know—animals, things that aren't human, animals.

HIM: Yeah, wild animals roamin' free—what was it—a wilderbeast do you think?

HER: That's what it was—a big screaming wilderbeast.

HIM: I definitely heard something—put the shit up ye noises like that.

HER: Maybe it was an owl, it could've been an owl.

HIM: Screamin'?

HER: I don't know—maybe owls scream, I don't know—you probably just imagined it.

HIM: I didn't.

HER: Alright you heard it—give me the gun and I'll go and shoot it.

HIM: That's not fuckin' funny.

HER: Sorry.

[*Silence*]

HIM: You any warmer?

HER: A bit—I'm tired.

HIM: Yeah.

HER: I wish I was home in my own bed.

HIM: Yeah.

HER: Maybe if we'd met in a pub or something earlier you'd be lying beside me.

HIM: Maybe.

HER: You'd have had to sneak out before my parents got up though—do you think we would have?

HIM: What?

HER: Ended up together—if we had met before the park bench do you think we would've ended up together?

HIM: I don't know—I don't care—what might've happened is of no interest to me at the moment, you understand.

HER: I'm just saying, talking, that's all.

HIM: Right.

HER: It would be nice to know if you would've liked me or not—well?

HIM: If I had nothing else to do on a wet, boring Friday afternoon I might've asked you to go to the pictures with me.

HER: Thank you.

HIM: Try and get some sleep.

HER: I can't.

HIM: I thought you were tired.

HER: I am but I can't sleep.

HIM: No.

[*Silence*]

HER: I spy with my little eye.

HIM: Stars.

HER: How'd you know that?

HIM: It's pitch black—the only thing we can see is stars.

HER: They're beautiful.

HIM: Yes.

HER: Just lying looking at them—when I was a child we used to go camping. [*Pause*] At night I'd sneak out of the caravan and just lie on my back and look up at them, just lie there for hours— used to wish I could sit on one of them, dangling my legs, looking down at everything below, not being part of it, just looking at it—you ever do that?

HIM: I think I did—not the stars though.

HER: What—what did you loose yourself in?

HIM: My ma used to bring us all to the beach now and again, just for the day—I would go off and find a place of my own and just sit and look out at the sea—don't know what it was, maybe because it was so big or something, I don't know.

HER: Freedom that's what it was—being alone and being free.

HIM: Freedom, what's that? Yesterday I was firing out hamburgers, I thought I was trapped, thought I was going nowhere, the whole fucking charade bored me to death—I wasn't trapped, I was free—now I'm trapped, trapped in some fucking forest with somebody I don't know and who's as frightened as I am.

HER: We're not trapped we'll get out of here—steal another car, get some money, a boat over to the continent, that's it.

HIM [*laughing*]: That simple is it?

HER: Yeah.

HIM: What are we going to do when we get there—people who make journey's have something in mind, an end result—we've nothing, fuck all—whatever it was you thought you were going to do in the world is fucking gone—scrubbed, finished, fucking gone.

HER: No it's not, stop talking like that—we're free.

HIM: Trapped.

HER: Shut up.

HIM: Trapped.

HER: Shut up. Right, we're back on the park bench, that's where we are, we're back on the park bench.

HIM: No park bench here.

HER: We're back on the park bench—so what is it, tell me, what is it you really want.

HIM: Not now—no, not now.

HER: We're on the park bench—what is it?

HIM: No.

HER: Right then I'll go. I want to be a teacher, I want to teach
history but not like it's taught in schools, not that nonsense—
history that's relevant, history that makes a difference to
people's lives. What you do is go into a small community and
set up your own place, nothing grand maybe just a room and
in that room show the history of that community, the history of
the people who live there, their history. Like instead of waffling
on about who started the First World War or whatever, tell it
through the eyes of the people who lived there, make it
practical, make it real. The outside world learns something
about their community and they learn something about
themselves. Nothing to do with bits of paper, documents,
meetings, men in suits behind closed doors. History about
their joys, heartbreaks, destruction, the building up of things
again. It would be like explaining where that community came
from and why it is the way it is. And the school wouldn't be for
children—no—for everyone, the history they would be learning
would be important because it would be about them. Right
your go now.

HIM: I want to have my own hamburger place—me—my place, no
jumped up little shit giving me orders, treating me like I know
fuck all about anything—my place—nothing like the normal
rip-off joints where they fire pieces of rubber at you in shit
coloured squeaky boxes—this place would have a bit of class
about it—your own table, someone to serve you, napkins, a real
wine list and none of that fucking cheap plastic cutlery, the
proper gear, the works, you know—I'd do all the cooking—go
out that morning and buy everything fresh, the best of stuff—
it would be like an open plan effort, you know, so all the
punters could see me doing the business, they order something
from the menu then see me cook it—no fucking about, you get
what you pay for—and then when I wasn't cooking I'd be out
on the floor, having a yarn with the customers, make them feel
at ease, make them feel like they're welcome—you know what
I'm saying, you create a good friendly atmosphere and they'll

always want to come back—it would be the same with the people that worked there, make them feel wanted, treat them well and everything's alright—I always had this notion too that there'd be music about the place you know—not that easy listening piped shite—a live band blasting out some serious tunes—have that in a wee room on its own, mightn't be everybody's cup of tea you know—and if the punters were lucky enough I might get up and give it a blast myself the odd night—it would be the type of place once you'd been there you'd remember it and want to go back—well fed, a good night out and I'm the man that owns it—that's it, that's what I want.

HER: A teacher and a chef—not much to ask for is it?

HIM: A chef that owns his own place—that's important, the owning your own place bit is important. Know what I've just thought you could combine the two couldn't you—mix the two areas together—listen to this, wherever we're going right, say it's Spain or Portugal or somewhere.

HER: Greece.

HIM: Aye Greece then—the two of us could set this place up in some wee village or whatever.

HER: What place?

HIM: It would be like say a building that you had divided into three—three separate things but all under the one roof—a hamburger joint, a music type place and then some sort of teaching area.

HER: Teaching what?

HIM: I don't know—alright say you learned the local history of the place, then you could have a museum type of thing—that's it—that would attract the interest of the locals and it would also be a touristy type of thing wouldn't it, they always want to know about the local gen—food, music, education, history, whatever, all under the one roof—it's ideas like that that work you know, something that nobody else has ever thought of.

HER: Maybe Greece isn't a good idea then, I know a bit more about Spain, I'd be happier with Spain.

HIM: Spain then—and once you're there it's not that hard to pick the lingo up—you're there, you're forced to use it, you pick it up.

HER: A big house with plenty of rooms—be better if you could get somewhere like that near the beach—you could have people staying there as well.

HIM: There'd have to be a kitchen in it.

HER: I know that—I know there'd have to be a kitchen.

[*The following morning—still in the forest*]

HER: Have we got everything, c'mon we're gonna have to move.

HER: I'm still half asleep—give me a second to get the sleep out of my eyes.

HIM: We want to get out of here now—it's daylight—time to go.

HER: Oh shit, look a wee bird must've fallen out of its nest. Must be injured it's flapping one of its wee wings. What will we do?

HIM: Leave it.

HER: I'm not leaving it like that.

HIM: Kill it then.

HER: We could leave it off at a vet somewhere.

HIM: Talk bloody sense.

HER: It's a wee bird.

HIM: Kill the fucking thing, put it out of its misery.

HER: A wee bird, it's tiny head with those wee tiny eyes, no chance, you kill it. You going to shoot it?

HIM: Start thinking straight will you—somebody would hear the shot wouldn't they?

HER: What then?

HIM: Hit it with a stone.

HER: Crush its wee head?

HIM: Hopefully yeah.

HER: You really going to do it.

HIM: It can't be left suffering.

HER: You really going to do it—really like?

HIM: Shut up or I'll hit you with the stone. [*Standing over bird*] You sure it can't fly?

HER: Try it.

HIM: Go on away you go, up, up, away, go on.

HER: Lift it.

HIM: I don't want to lift it.

HER: It's only a bird.

HIM: I know that's why I don't want to lift it. Alright, alright—bloody thing gives me the willies. [*Bird in hands*] Right son this is your chance—it's this or the death march kid—go for it. [*The bird flies away.*] What about that hey, Francis of Assisi I am.

HER: Away you go birdy, fly away home.

HIM: Home, fly home

[*They stare at each other in silence.*]

HIM: C'mon let's go.

[*In the car. Music up. Music down. Mid-conversation.*]

HER: There's bound to be a wee garage up the road that'll do. I just think we should pay for the food that's all.

HIM: Rob the place but pay for the food.

HER: Yes.

HIM: Strange value system you have.

HER: If you're buying something you pay for it, if you're stealing something you steal it.

HIM: Oh right—I was thinkin' about Portugal.

HER: Spain.

HIM: Aye Spain—I don't know if I like the idea about people stayin' in the place.

HER: It means they would have everything under the one roof—that was your idea, everything under the one roof.

HIM: I know that.

HER: Be like a complex.

HIM: I know I understand that—it's just you'd have to be lookin' after them all the time, there'd be no rest, you'd be trapped in the bloody place—plus it would only be tourists staying, locals mightn't like that, might put them off coming to the place.

HER: Have it like a hostel then, let them do their own thing.

HIM: That might work now, put them in another building or something—aye that might be it.

HER: There's a garage up ahead.

HIM: A hostel, yeah that sounds right—have to think about that later.

HER: Right, let's get our act together here. What are we going to get to eat?

HIM: I don't know, food?

HER: Work it out before we go in, we don't want to be hanging about.

HIM: Milk, cheese.

HER: I'm allergic to dairy products.

HIM: No dairy products—lemonade and crisps then.

HER: Except cheese and onion.

HIM: Bread, that alright?

HER: Of course it is.

HIM: You might be allergic to bread, how do I know.

HER: Ever hear of anyone allergic to bread?

HIM: No.

HER: Well then.

HIM: Never heard of anyone allergic to dairy products either. You not eat custard then?

HER: No.

HIM: Shit, I love custard, couldn't go through life without custard.

HER: Lemonade, bread and crisps.

HIM: No butter.

HER: No.

HIM: Fuck sake. Right you gather up all that shit and pay for it. I'll produce the bad news, get the readies from the till and we're out of there.

HER: Ready.

HIM: Deep breath.

HER: Deep breath.

HIM: Let's go. Wait a minute.

HER: What?

HIM: Is the safety catch on this?

HER: I don't know.

HIM: I've been tossin' it about like fuckin' Roy Rogers and the safety catch isn't on?

HER: I said I don't know.

HIM: Did you put it on?

HER: Did you put it on?

HIM: Jesus Christ—I don't want the fuckin' thing goin' off—we go in, get the money, get out, that's it nothing else. That's it there—I think.

HER: Be careful.

HIM: Aye that's it—right let's go.

[*Enter garage*]

HIM: Hello, how you doing. I heard that—sunny for the rest of the week. No, that right, all dead? Catch anyone? Combing the countryside—I imagine they would be. Have you got everything dear?

HER: Nearly dear.

HIM [*pointing gun*]: There's nothing to panic about, just go to the till and give us whatever's in it. No hurdy gurdy stuff and no one will get hurt. Nice and easy that's you.

HER [*to* HIM]: Excuse me. [*To shopkeeper*] Have you no other crisps than cheese and onion?

HIM: Fuck the crisps. [*To shopkeeper*] Just you keep going.

HER: Lemonade and bread, we need more than lemonade and bread.

HIM [*to shopkeeper*]: Women what? [*To* HER] There's ham over there, take that.

HER: I'm a vegetarian.

HIM: Fish?

HER: No.

HIM: What do you live on—fucking fresh air?

HER: Vegetables, fruit.

HIM [*to shopkeeper*]: You're doing a great job. [*To* HER] Then lift some.

HER: Do you like bananas?

HIM: I'm going to fucking shoot you. [*To shopkeeper*] Don't panic—
not you, her.

HER: Bananas?

HIM: Yes, fucking yes.

HER [*to shopkeeper*]: How much is that? Two fifty seven, shit that's
dear. [*To* HIM] Any change, I've only a fiver.

HIM: Give him the fucking money.

HER: I've only—

HIM: The money—give it to him.

HER [*to shopkeeper*]: That's why no one comes in here, you're too
dear.

HIM: I've just thought of something. [*To shopkeeper*] Just stand
there, don't fucking move and shut the fuck up. [*He releases the
safety catch on the gun.*]

HER: What?

HIM: He's seen our faces he knows what we look like.

HER: Oh shit.

HIM: Fuck it.

   [*They stand motionless looking at the audience.*]

I WON'T DANCE DON'T ASK ME
(1993)

I Won't Dance Don't Ask Me was first performed in the Ulster Arts Club Belfast on 15th November 1993. The role of Gus McMahon was played by Sean Caffrey. The production was also directed by Sean Caffrey. Produced by Who The Hell Theatre Company.

Empty stage but for an armchair drapped with two or three sheets of wallpaper. Surrounding the armchair is a square of light (representing a room) outside of which the actor should not step. The only other prop (optional) is a bottle of Guinness.

It's 4 o'clock in the morning GUS MCMAHON *can't sleep. He is in the living room of his house with his 'cat' Sparky. Gus' wife and son are both asleep upstairs.*

Are you listening sleepers? Fuck you and the wallpaper—wallpaper my fuck. Sparky cat—having a sleep pets—did the wallpaper trick disturb you pets? Livers? Does my Sparky pet want some livers? Livers for my pets. You must let them know, Sparky, make them listen.

She thought I'd balls it up you see. I would, but that's not the point. She's working, I'm not. She papers the room, that makes me look bad. She wasn't thinking, when people aren't thinking you must let them know. Remember that, Sparky—the old thought trick. People don't think, then they listen to other people who don't think, that's what's wrong, no thinking. We know, Sparky, don't we—think.

The boy doesn't think. The boy. The sample. Always have more than one—alone too often you see, it affects their mind. I'm standing in the kitchen pouring soup into a pot, Guinness and oyster, good stuff. I put a drop of water in the tin and fire it into the pot. "You shouldn't do that," he says, "the soup's ready as it is." Do you understand that Sparky, do you understand a mind that works like that? It's my soup—if I wanted to have a Lilian Gish in the pot it's up to me, isn't it? You know what he does though, he puts the tops back on empty milk bottles then puts them back in the fridge—who in their right fucking mind does that? He says to me there's no God, the world's made up solely of atoms and that my generation are emotionally retarded and he puts the tops back on empty fucking milk bottles. Those wee silver chats you just throw away—if there's an empty milk bottle in your fridge you tell it to get out to fuck and make way for the full chats.

Are you the only one that listens to me, Sparky? This morning. That's it, this morning. The three of us were sitting round the breakfast table this morning. Bread, butter, jam, toast, cornflakes, tea, coffee, orange juice—bliss. She was dressed for work, blue suit, important looking, and the boy was waiting on his lift to College, dressed like an out of work poet. "Maybe we could meet for lunch in town, my treat." "Yeah, I've only one lecture this afternoon, metaphysics and its analysis. Yeah, about half-one." "Make it earlier, I've a meeting with my head of department at two." "Is there any milk left?" (Must remember to buy some.) Nothing. I've nothing worth saying so they don't listen. "Bye Gus." "I'm here, I'm sitting at the table." "Bye, bye, bye—don't forget the milk." Vanished, time to go. I'm alone. I just sat there, couldn't move, didn't want to move, stuck rigid. I'm stirring at the tea pot too long, it goes blurred then everything in the room's up close to me. Close my eyes, drifting off. Then I saw a mountain and I was standing at the bottom of it and it was raining, round balls of rain, perfect round balls and I had no coat on. What the fuck's happening to me? The boy thinks I drink too much. What do you reckon, Sparky? He doesn't know what he's talking about, he doesn't know the story. It's about who I am, what I did. He thinks it's enough to call me Gus—I know who you are because we're on first name terms—no, there's more to it than that. Drink and the betting game go hand-in-hand—bacon and eggs, brandy and a good cigar. When I started up I had a choice, learn from those who know or become a pencil-stealer, a clock-watcher, a nine-to-five—"I obey the rules, yes sir, I do." You see those people are small, petty-minded, dishonest tosspots hiding behind whatever rule, regulation, document, decision, fucking lie they're told to. It was like that then and it's the same now. It's all logos, value for money, computer print outs, nice spongy black sofas—what about people, nobody thinks in terms of people anymore. It's all a million miles an hour—no time, no time just eat lunch at your desk. I always wanted to stay clear of that you see. Have a drink, get to know people, make the whole think social, give it a meaning—fuck what time it is, make this part of your life, not just a job, there's no sense to it then. Drink was all part of that—race meetings, the dogs, clerking for some fella who'd pay you over the odds if he won, point-to-points, coarsing, whatever it was—just make it more then pay cheques and stealing fucking pencils. It was personal to me, that's the thing—it was personal.

How do you explain that to them when they're sitting down to lunch talking about department meetings and metaphysics? How do you do that? Lunch. I was overlooked on that one. I don't eat lunch anymore, Sparky, do you know that? I haven't earned it so I can't eat it. Lunch is for workers, people who work eat lunch, and I don't work. I don't work. "Sure don't you look after the house Gus." That's it. I'm 54 and I look after the house—that's it, dusting shelves, scraping pots and folding sheets. I must be the fucking envy of the western world—what an idyllic little life. That can't be what I end up with—it isn't right—it's not fair. When she comes home form work what have I got to tell her—of what importance is it?

"Did you have a nice day?" "Yes, so did I." "Any post?" "A letter from the club book." "Chops for dinner?" "Chops for dinner." "Oh, by the way, after you left this morning I drank a few bottles of Guinness and read the obituaries. Did you know our milkman's sister died in a car crash? It's awful sad, she left three young children behind and a husband who's an alcoholic. Not that that makes him a bad person you understand. Oh, I forgot to tell you the grocer's doing a special on watermelons this week, so I bought 36 fucking dozen, just in case. I left some of those nice chocolate biscuits you like in the cupboard."

What type of thoughts are they to fill your head with? And then the boy says, "Why don't you read some Jean Paul Sartre, enlighten yourself." That's a bit of a fucking leap Sparky isn't it—chocolate bickies and watermelons to Jean Paul Sartre.

Enlighten my mind. Jesus. Oh, I'm enlightened alright. The boy's getting married soon, right. Right. He's still a student—not a pot to piss in but that's his business. Thirty years I've been married. Does he ask me anything—no. I know—if I know he must know that's my responsibility—it's a duty, my duty.

"You won't get this from a book, boy." Always carrying books, end up with arms like one of those pink-arsed monkey chats. "What do you reckon about this marriage trick—have you given it any thought, what do you reckon?"

"It'll be alright."

"What do you really know about it?"

"Nothing, I haven't been married yet."

"Do you want to know what it's all about, I'll tell you will I. I'll do that for you. Have you ever seen your girlfriend go to the toilet—no—well that's what marriage is all about." Blank face—"I'm trying to tell you something here, listen."

And then he's away.

Romantic notions—it's my job to get rid of those, Sparky, it's not right to think like that. You marry a person not an image—it's important to know that so I told him. If Jean Paul Sartre or Plato or one of those other head up the metropole people had have told him that—no but because it was me. I just didn't want him to look at her one day and realise he didn't know her—all that time wasted, it's no good.

Reality Sparky, not myths. Robert Redford should have been a bastard with bad teeth, that would have sorted all this out—he should have beat the cleevers out of his wife, whored about and generally fucked things up, that would have destroyed the image, made things easier for everyone. A picture of Jane Fonda first thing in the morning, boking her ring up after being out on the piss all night, that's what we want. But no—a touch of romance a quick bit of the old cough rock and life will be hunky-dory for ever and a day. The Yanks have it all sussed. Movieland that's where we live—the world's one big MGM fucking studio. The world's your oyster, bigger is better, look after yourself, happy ending. That's how I lost my job you know, the bigger the better conspiracy has filtered down. Expansion is the way forward, it's the only answer. And if you don't like it *hasta la viste* baby.

Twenty years I managed that bookies, then bang it's sold—too small, need to expand, new staff, all young—bright-eyed, bushy-tailed, shiny hair and floppy suits. "Thank you, here's a framed photocopy of a print of some horse called Arkle." That'll not happen to Robert Redford will it? What does my wife say, Sparky—what little pearl of wisdom does she come off with? "Sure you need the rest Gus, you've been working all your life—take it easy." That's when I knew, once she uttered those words I knew—*You don't know who I am do you?* I'm a worker, that's all I do, I don't know anything else. Why do you think I can't hang fucking wallpaper?

When I worked, Sparky—when I worked I was in control—I had a place in this world and it was inside that betting shop—I was an artist. I used to write up a meeting on the blackboard and stand back and just stare at it and all the time I was thinking Christ I'm good, there's no one does that better than me. It wasn't much but I was the best. It was like looking in a mirror, I could see myself in my own handwriting. I looked at it, I recognised it and I knew it was me. That's been taken away from me, do you understand what I'm saying, Sparky, it's gone—I turned my back and some person who wants to make their mark in the world because they've been told that's the right thing to do, makes a decision about my life. Someone who doesn't know me made a decision about my life. That's not right. Decisions behind closed doors—that's where we're at. Whisper, whisper and keep that door shut. All doors must be shut—they're on the inside, you're on the outside.

I went back today, Sparky—went back. I needed to see some familiar faces, slap on the back—"The place isn't the same without you, Gus." I don't know why I wanted that—maybe it was the thing at the breakfast table—the old round balls of rain trick, Sparky. We always want to go back—the past's there, inviting us to dance and just as you've finished putting your top hat and tails on the music stops. It's all in the head, Sparky pets—the past's all in the napper.

I walked straight in through the door and nothing. I didn't recognise anything. It used to be a small place no bigger than this room—the punters all huddled together. There where blackboards on two of the walls and the other two where covered in newspapers. The place was always littered with dockets, in the background the radio'd be blurting out the commentary. Newmarket, Chepstow, Uttoxeter, Kelso, Doncaster, The Curragh. The one-fifty-five at Newmarket, seven furlongs, the going's good-to-soft. They're at the six furlong marker—"Brave Boy and Our Rita followed by Parliament Piece. Brave Boy and Our Rita—Brave Boy—come on my son, lift them pinkie." I turned to look at the boards, compare the writing you know, but they weren't there, just TV screens. Each one had the runners of a race on them, then the word off would flash up and when the race was over the screen would change and the result would appear. No horses, no jockeys, no race, just words. This was a lifeless place with no soul. I looked around for faces I knew and spotted one so I walked over to him. "Did you get the last winner?" "Nah, I backed the second co." Then he turned away and got on with the business

of picking his next loser. I used to have a gargle with this man.
When he was short of a few quid I'd let him have a bet and he'd
pay me at the weekend. I knew him and now he didn't know how
to talk to me. He had things to do, Sparky pets, his own life to lead.
I wasn't part of that anymore. Do you understand that, I was of no
use to him so he didn't want to know. He didn't want to know.

Then it happened again. Everybody was moving, it felt like they
were all coming towards me—their mouths opening and closing
but no noise. "I'm here, look at me I'm here"—the words, inside
my head, I kept thinking I have to get them out—they can't stay
there forever I have to get them out. I closed my eyes, I felt
everyone moving around me. It's all blurred and spinning,
spinning. I can't move, legs like lead weights. I'm beginning to
sweat. "I'm here, I'm fucking here—can't you see me?" Everything
stopped, no action just like the TV screens. Standing rigid. "Are
you alright, son?"—some old man in front of me—a big red face,
right up close. "Must leave, must leave now." Then I was back in
the street and it was over. If I was to tell that to the boy he'd explain
it in molecules and chemical reactions. Fuck that. Have you
finished your livers, Sparky? That's it, you give yourself a good
wash.

I'm not going mad. I'm not, there's just some things I don't
understand. Can you be married for thirty years and not know if
you love the woman you're married to? Then there's the boy. I
told him he was incapable of loving someone. "I think you're
incapable of loving someone," I said. Jesus. He just kept staring at
me. I could see it in his face. "Why do you want to hurt me?" That's
what he was thinking. And I was thinking because you're my son.
I'm angry and I need to cut someone and you're the only one left.
You're on the way up and I'm on the way down and sometimes
that's difficult to take. There were no words after that. I should've
explained to him but I didn't. It's me—do you hear that it's me,
not you—there's something happening here and I don't know

what it is—but it's me, not you. You see, Sparky—I can't explain things to people, to him—I never could.

When the boy was about 12 he was playing a football match, it was the first time he was picked for the school team. It was important. I wanted to be there. This was my chance to be there for him. I was always busy with work and that you know, not that I was one of those ambitious pushy types, it's just what I did. His mother bought him new boots, he didn't want them, embarrassed in front of his mates I suppose, but she insisted. He was full of energy, chasing everything, running himself into the ground, eager to do well—maybe just having fun. "That's it son, you show them, take no prisoners, kid." Him and another boy were running for the ball—head on towards each other, "Go on boy, you can do it, go on, go on." Just at the last second he pulled away from the tackle. He was taken off after that. I followed him into the dressing room. He was sitting on a bench looking at the new boots, the ones he didn't want in case he didn't play well and then the rest of the team would all say to him "Why'd your ma buy you boots when you can't play football?" Do you know what I said to him Sparky, do you know what I said— "Nice pair of boots." No pat on the back and hard luck kid. No, there'll be other matches son don't worry. Nice pair of boots. You have to learn to talk to people, it doesn't come natural, you got to work at it. I was too busy then and now I don't know how, so it's all no water in the soup and tops on empty fucking milk bottles.

Do you know what I think, Sparky pets? I think there's something in the water that's making us all go ga-ga. That's what happens you know, no sweat about it. "Are you thirsty, take that wee cup of water" and all of a sudden the head's gone.

Do you know anyone that's wise? No! Everyone's napper's gone. You think you have one, you're talking away to someone and you think this is it, here we are, the only sane person I know and then you realise they're wearing slip-ons and white socks and then you take another look and the trousers are too short or the head starts twitching or they start smelling their food and then you think hold on here what's going on? In a couple of years' time we'll all be sitting in front of the TV gulping down pints of water while waiting for the special fried rice to be delivered. There'll be no need to go outside the house, just plug your computer into the TV, do your work, then order whatever clothes or food you need. Everybody will be selling something, one big market place— that'll be their job. Every product will be multi-purpose—inflatable rubber tea towels you can use as picture frames and if taken short, wipe your arse with—brief cases you fold inside out and use as deep sea diving suits. I flicked the TV on the other day Sparky and this happy woman of about fifty, with teeth like a snow blizzard, who had just climbed the south face of K2 barefoot or crossed the Atlantic in a shoe box or something, was telling me this new shampoo would do wonders for my hair. It had a dye in it that was the natural colour of your hair but better. Better? What the fuck does that mean? It's not better it's just different that's all. And then there's some poor bugger's sitting by their electric fire, which only has one bar on because they're skint, watching this and thinking I wonder should I improve the gingerness of my hair? So they buy it, use it and stand in front of the mirror and think, "Yes. I am complete. I am ready for the world today and is my hair ginger or what. My life's going to change, I know it, lets go." It's a lie, they're being told a lie. Nothing's going to change. In another ten minutes that one bar's going to go out and they're going to be freezing the rest of the day. No K2, no Atlantic ocean, no excitement just different colour hair and a cold house.

I've gone the other way now Sparky pets, I can't believe anything. I can't read the newspaper, can't watch television. I've stopped listening to people I don't know and those I do know I only half listen to. It wasn't meant to be like this—this wasn't the picture I had. I always thought that things would be clearer the older I got but they're not. I can't make decisions anymore. Today I was standing in the bakery—gravy rings 23p for one or 5 for 99p, jam doughnuts 29p for one or 4 for 99p. I shouldn't know that, I'm 54 and I know the price of gravy rings and jam doughnuts. How many men my age know the price of those things? I should be in work where I belong. I'm standing at the counter, it's my turn and the woman's looking at me, pissed off because she put her washing out this morning before she came to work and now it's belting down and she's going to have to do it all again and no one's going to thank her for it.

"What do you want?"

"I don't know."

"This is a bakery."

"A jam doughnut. No, a gravy ring."

"What do you normally get?"

"I alternate, today's gravy ring day."

"A gravy ring then?"

"Why not a jam doughnut?"

"I don't know."

"Neither do I."

I used to be responsible for the running of a business and now I can't decide between two friggin' buns. I tried to tell her about the doughnut thing but it was no use, she didn't understand what I was talking about, what I was saying. You know what she said to me, Sparky? She said, "Why didn't you buy currant squares?" I don't like currant squares, we've been married thirty years and she doesn't know I don't like currant squares.

"I don't like them."

"I thought you did."

"When have you ever seem me eat one?"

"I can't remember."

"Before we were married we were in your house, in the parlour, your mother came in with tea and currant squares—'Would you like a currant square, Gus?' 'No, thank you, I don't like them'— can't you remember, it isn't that long ago?"

"I've a report to fill in, Gus. Can we discuss this later?"

You see, she has more important things to think about that's why she can't remember—but me I've plenty of time so I remember everything, every useless, unimportant stupid detail. "Would you like a currant square, Gus?" "No, thank you, I don't like them." I don't want to remember things like that, that isn't what I want in my head. They just appear, rattling around in there.

When I was 16 I went to the pictures to see *The Ladykillers*. Alec Guinness and Peter Sellers where in it. I sat on some chewing gum and it ruined my good trousers. What's the point in knowing that—what's it doing there? If I'd have been in work and that thought had flashed by I'd have said "Get to fuck out. I've other things to do, people are depending on me." Row F, third seat over from the centre. Two rows ahead, directly in front of me was a man and woman in their mid-forties, they talked the whole way through the picture. At the interval I bought an ice-cream and a bag of lemon *bon-bons*. Alec Guinness played the head of a gang of bank robbers. His landlady found out so they tried to kill her but all their attempts back-fired. When I left the cinema it was raining. So what?

Alec Guinness? Jesus! Never liked him, he can act none. Arthur Guinness—that's my man. A bottle of Guinness and a Johnny Walker Black, nothing else. That's how you break the back of it—don't change your drink. Always stick to the same gear and your swanny river will stay the course and distance. And no smoking—I keep telling people cut the oily regs out, they're no good—a killer. You must look after yourself. I can still do press ups, Sparky, did you know that? Oh yes and the correct way too, none of this starting off laying down business. Stand straight, arms out in front of you, drop to the floor and right into them.

[*He does this, collapsing when he hits the floor. He stays there out of breath.*]

I used to be able to do it but you didn't know me then, Sparky.
[*He sits up, puts his legs straight out and tries to touch his toes. Fails. He feels a sharp pain in his back.*]
Jesus Christ. Pain's good for the soul, Sparky pets—good for the soul.
[*He crawls to the chair and pulls himself onto it.*]
It is, my fuck. [*Silence*]

Do cats get prostrate problems—do they, Sparky? Have you started to piss in instalments? I can't sleep anymore because I keep thinking I'm going to wet the bed. I doze off about five in the morning, then I'm up again at seven—work time. I was always an early riser. The other night I fired a lot of Guinness and Benelyn into me—knock me out. I wet the bed. After 54 years I'm starting to piss the bed. She didn't say anything, I admire her for that. She could've made a big deal out of it. Maybe she was thinking, "I'm married to an animal, who soaks our bed with his own piss." She didn't say it though. I spent the whole day with the mattress propped against the wall and the hair dryer on. "Just tighten the muscles in your buttocks when you're urinating, Mr. McMahon." Thank you doctor. Brilliant. Now I'm going to end up with an arse as tight as a pinhole. I'm frightened, Sparky, that frightens me. No.
[*He takes a small bottle from his pocket and sniffs the contents.*]

The old smelling salts trick—keep the head right. Ballroom dancing—the good old ballroom dancing, that's the business. What do you know, Sparky, about the old one, two, three, one, two, three? "Why don't we take a night class in ballroom dancing, Gus?" Very perceptive my wife—she sees there's something not quite right and being the good lady she is wants to help. A bolt of lightning, a stroke of genius, ballroom fucking dancing.

I used to be a pretty good mover too—jiving that was my thing. Now her thing you see is night classes—anything and everything.

Advancing her mind slowly by degrees. A computer class here, a flower arranging class there. Yoga, tank maintenance, build your own house. She made that pretty little vase over there—now I couldn't do that, that's not my bag as they say. She also mentioned swimming and driving but only in passing. Maybe she thought they were a bit too advanced for me at the moment. I know, I know what you're thinking, I should do these things, keep myself active, join in. But you see, Sparky, I thought I could get through life avoiding them, that's what I had prepared myself for. But I've been caught. A spotlight is glaring down on me and picking me out as a waster because all the others thrown on the shit heap, redundancy, paid off, business bust or whatever, they're all swimming and driving in their droves. People who fainted in the bath or couldn't sit in the back of a taxi without spewing are now all Johnny Weissmuller and Graham fucking Hill. All these things are starting to build up now you see—I can't hang wallpaper, I can't swim, I can't drive and I won't learn to waltz. Where would I drive to? Where would I swim to? Where would I waltz to?

I never wanted to swim—if I had've I would've—that hasn't changed. Would I be cured doing length after length after meaningless length? No, then fuck it. Would it make me any more productive in the world? No, then fuck it. Would I gain people's respect by swimming? No, but it's not even that you see, Sparky— if I start doing those things it means I've given in. I'll have accepted that I'm no longer of any use in the real world so I'll spend my time waltzing and swimming and maybe I'll combine the two and go for that synchronised bollocks. No, not me, not yet, not ever. Not Gus McMahon. No. They won't do that to me, I won't be forced to spend my life doing things I never wanted to do. I don't want to make a vase and she can't make me. Do you hear that? No vases. No wallpaper and no fucking vases.

Ballroom dancing, I think they should put it on the National Health, Sparky pets. "Next please. What's wrong with you? Off the rocker is it—I've booked you in for five sessions down at the Plaza, that'll sort you out. Having problems with your bladder? I've just the thing—nurse the jitter bug music." Everything's geared towards making you feel worthless—a burden. I had to make an appointment to sign on and then I was referred to as one of their clients.

"Do you want to work, Mr. McMahon?"

"I'd prefer to go on a world cruise but with readies being tight and that—maybe that's something you could sort out for me."

"You're at a difficult age you understand, you have valuable hands on experience—it's a pity you weren't ten years younger."

"I'm sorry I can't help you, it's this ageing process thing I can't seem to be able to shake it."

"The only thing we have at the moment, and again it's for a younger person, is a trainee computer programmer. We could of course put you on a government sponsored training programme in either the building or engineering industries. If we get anything else we'll let you know and remember we're always only an appointment away."

You see the guy who was dealing with me, his handwriting was like a child's—he couldn't spell co-ordinate. It's a joke. I couldn't see under the table but I could feel the vibes drifting up from his slip-ons. I kept thinking I hope this happens to you someday kid. I want you to sit in this seat and be humiliated by some ... you're right, he's only trying to earn a living.

Readies, money, money, money. What would you think the chances would be of me walking down a street in New York and going into one of these take-away places and ordering a bowl of Irish stew or an Ulster Fry. It's funny that isn't it—I can cross the street here and buy a big bucket of that Kentucky Fried shite though. We start off with pieces of chicken and end up destroying everything of value—bigger, better, faster. No time for people— people are scrubbed, stroked off the list of tasks to complete—

potential fulfilling tasks. "Today was a bad day, I did not fulfil my potential. I must see my analyst about this and make sure he fulfils his potential." And we fall for it—we're told this is the way to live and eventually we go for it. I should have taken myself off to the U S of A and opened up a chain of stew take-aways. "And how would you like your stew sir, on a plate or the Irish way—in a coal bucket on the back of a donkey?" And then I could have a special—"Buy your child a mini-bucket of stew and you'll get completely free of charge a small plastic thatched cottage complete with ginger-haired, better than her own natural ginger of course, maiden colleen, wearing an Aran sweater knitted by her drunken granny while in front of an open turf fire, boiling a field-and-a-half of potatoes. Yes and you have a nice day too."

Why didn't we go to America when we were first married—we could have been big now in Kentucky. The boy'd be in college now studying golf course management—happy days. I must talk with him—I need to do that. "Why don't you go swimming with Mom, you might enjoy it?" No first name terms there. "I don't like the water it's too wet." "Water isn't actually wet—to say water is wet doesn't describe any quality that the water has—water is wet is inaccurate—water is water." I don't understand that and that's what's inside his head. Water on the brain. Ha, ha, ha. I don't care about the water, forget the water. I love you. I love you.

I can't say it, I never could. I've never said those words to anyone. Does that make me a bastard, Sparky, do you think? Emotionally retarded, maybe the boy's right. I'll give you whatever odds you like the boyos in slip-ons have no problem saying it—"What would you like for breakfast dear?" "A boiled egg beat up in a cup and cut the toast into little soldiers. I love you." "I love you too." "Not as much as I love you—I love you the equivalent of a Citybus full of Ballyhornan sand each grain being an ocean of love. Good morning children—oh wife of mine and mother of my children beat up eggs and soldiers all round. I love you all."

I remember going to the hospital when the boy was born and holding him in my arms. Hannah was sleeping—the three of us together and I thought I'm happy, this is the way it's meant to be. And then *whoosh* I'm here. The *whoosh* factor. I've a dummy in my mouth then *whoosh* I'm playing handball at the bottom of the street then *whoosh* I'm working then *whoosh* I'm married then *whoosh* I'm a father then *whoosh* I'm ... what am I?

I came straight back to the house after the bookies thing—folded every sheet, every towel, washed every dish. Sat in this room, turned the TV on—racing Epsom. Who won the Derby in 1966—you don't know—a lot of good philosophy is boy. I know though—Charlottown, 25th May 1966. A horse called Anglo won the Grand National that year. What use is it knowing that—it's like the chewing gum on the arse of the trousers—no use—TV off. I couldn't sit in the room, the wallpaper was annoying me—I had to get out. So I got onto a bus and headed for the nearest swimming pool, had a swim and then had a session on the sunbed—the old sun tan trick.

That was a wee joke, Sparky pets. I went to the pub. I'm there in the middle of everyone holding court—that's me a bar-room philosopher—maybe that's where the boy gets it from. The drink's flying and it's all "Queen Victoria was a lesbian and knew fuck all about horse racing—*On The Waterfront* was the best movie every made—the Tories are a shower of shite—how can you walk from here to the Albert Clock without turning right?" All good stuff. I'm in control there Sparky you see—I know the lay of the land. The pub's like a commune, if you have it you spend it, if you don't you'll be looked after—that's the way things should be, if someone's in diffs, sort them out—there for the grace of God go I—or whatever. Today was different though. Someone had just ordered a drink. We were arguing about sex before marriage and I said, "Heavy petting's alright but don't follow through with the old cough rock." They all started to laugh and it got louder and louder—their faces getting bigger as if they were going to burst. Then it started happening again. The laughter, louder, louder. I thought oh Jesus no, not here—I've nowhere else to go. It's not that funny, stop laughing. Stop the laughing. They're all laughing at me. Gus the joker.

It's all racing through my head now—"He's a lazy fucker why doesn't he get a job—he drinks the grocery money you know—he has it made living off his wife—he's funny like but you couldn't take him seriously, you couldn't trust him with something important, like a job." Stop fucking laughing.

Where do you go when you want to think, Sparky—do you have a special place you wonder off to and get your act together? I ended up in the park. I don't know why, I was walking and then I'm sitting on a bench watching some children playing on the swings. I thought I'd like to do that. Why shouldn't I have a swing, it's not a crime. They all looked happy you see—I thought maybe it's the swinging that's making them happy. I was half-way over to them too—bloody stupid. Gus on the swings—the head has gone it's official—Gus McMahon has finally entered the twilight zone. My da painted the railings round the park—I bet you didn't know that, Sparky. Wee Mick the red leader.

There was a man knew his place in the world, no confusion there. Breakfast, work, dinner, paper, smoking, bed. Breakfast, work, dinner, paper, smoking, bed, drunk all weekend—then the same again. Never a word out of him to, unless he was gargled, then he'd curse the world up and down. He was a robot. There's only one thing I ever remember him doing or saying outside his routine. I was about 14. I was sitting in the house. It was a Saturday morning. "Why aren't you out playing handball, kid?" I was always playing against the gable wall at the bottom of the street. I was good too—best in the district. "I've no one to play with, they're all away at a football match." "I'll play you." And he did. We must have been down there playing for about two or three hours. Wee Mick, shirt sleeves rolled up, the sweat lashing out of him. It was the only time I ever saw him run or sweat or laugh or slap me on the back and say, "Well done, kid." After that it was back to the breakfast, work, dinner business. One morning's handball and I thought he was a great fella. One morning out of all that time.

Whenever my mother died there was just me and him for a while. "Have you my piece made up, kid?—get me twenty *Woodbine*, kid—I'm just going for a pint, kid—are those shoes polished, kid?" Grey fucking shoes. A grey men in grey shoes. He died six months after he retired. I was away at a race meeting, The Curragh or something. I walked into the house, nobody there—the coffin was in the parlour. Best suit and grey shoes. I took the shoes off and threw them in the bin and put mine on him. Grey shoes— they never just looked right. There lived a man and now he's dead and that was it. Grey isn't a colour you see, Sparky—it's bland, there's no life in it, it says nothing. And I believe you can tell a person by their shoes. Well it makes sense to me. We all live our lives by rules and theories we don't understand so why not another one. The Gus McMahon theory of grey shoes—people who wear grey shoes aren't worth a fuck.

Today was a journey Sparky but it didn't end in the park. I went to the gable wall—I didn't know that's where I was going but that's where I ended up. There was no one there so I went to the shop, bought a ball and had a game of handball. Whack whack whoosh. "Well done, kid." Serve, side of the hand, high against the wall, it'll go over his head. Dad runs backwards, stoops down to his left, scoops it up. Close the fist, smack it as low as you can. He's running as fast as he can—red face, puffing, panting—fist clenched— crack—below the brick.

   "Why are you stopping kid?"
   "That was below the brick."

"There's something wrong with your eyes. It's my serve give me the ball. What's the score?"

"Ten, nine to me."

"What wins it?"

"First to eleven."

"This is it then."

Dad serves—out of bounds.

"You've another go."

He serves high I can get it but I let it go.

"What's wrong with you? I thought you said you were good at this."

"Serve—ten all."

Serves high—whack—it's low—whack—high, low, low, high—whack whack—whack. Low and hard, I'm running for it—I'm going to reach it—it's there. Out of the corner of my eye I see the lamp post—I'm getting close to it, I'm going to smack into it. Go for the shot and hit the lamp post or stop. Go for the shot and hit the lamp post or stop.

"Go for the winner, kid."

I pull back. Stop. "Hindrance."

"No chance, kid, you could've got it. If you want to win you've got to go for your shots, kid."

Lying bastard, you lying bastard. You can't win anymore.

All my shots are out of date now, they're playing a new game and I don't even know the rules. I let you win you see—you weren't really up to it so I let you win—but they don't do that anymore. I walked up the street and stood outside my old house—journey's end. A small dingy wee place. I called at the door and said to the woman who answered it, "I used to live here—I played handball with my father at the bottom of the street—do you mind if I come in and have a look around—I just want to see how things have changed." "I'm afraid not."—door closed.

What was I doing there? That's what's frightening me, Sparky. I'm doing things and I don't know why. All the days from here on in can't be like this. When I was working I was alright but now it's all swings, paranoia, spontaneous deafness and playing handball with a man that's been dead for twenty fucking years.

You see Sparky, it's not me, I can't handle it, life hasn't equipped me for this. I don't want to delve deep, discover things I'd forgotten, unlock all the dreams, nightmares, guilt, longings that are bedded deep in my mind—that just fucks things up. It's too late for all that—I've lived a life, I'm used to it. Changing it won't do me any good. And this is it you see. If my da had never uttered a word to me in his whole life—what differences does it make to me? I'm a grown man now—what? I'm responsible for who I am that's the way it's always been. But you see, Sparky, when you've time on your hands you start thinking about these things and everything gets jumbled up. You start examining yourself and then you look at your family and think "Who am I? Who are they? Do they know me, do I know them?" And then you think why are they the way they are, is it my fault? I can't talk to my son because my father didn't talk to me. I don't love my wife and she doesn't care about me because I've been married for thirty years and she doesn't know I don't like currant squares—that's all bollocks. Not talking, talking too much, saying the wrong thing, saying the right thing, caring, not caring, loving, hating, comforting, arguing— that's the way things are, I can handle that, I understand it.

But when you've time on your hands it all becomes something else. You've nothing to do with your mind so you start asking questions—the questions become serious—you make up answers—connect things that aren't connected—then bang you're knocking at the door of your old house thinking this is going to help me, everthing's going to become clear, I'll understand. But you don't because it's all to do with today—now. That's why tomorrow can't be like today, something has to turn up you see or I'll keep asking the questions and it'll destroy me.

Is my Sparky pets asleep? Tomorrow will be different. I'll take up ballroom dancing [*starts to waltz*] *one, two, three, one, two, three.* Are you listening, you have to listen. *One, two, three, one, two, three ...*
[*Stage darkens*]

THE PRIVATE PICTURE SHOW
(1994)

The Private Picture Show was first perfomed at the Lyric Players' Theatre, Belfast, on 22nd November 1994. It was directed by Robin Midgley. The cast was as follows:

Iggy, *a 38 year-old writer*	Peter O'Meara
Lizzy, *a 54 year-old woman whose appearance*	
is that of a has-been cabaret singer	Barbara Adair
Beanpole, *a 44 year-old hippie*	
with his hair in a ponytail	Niall Cusack
Jimmy, *a 68 year-old ex-barman*	Birdy Sweeney
Linda, *a 30 year-old photo-journalist*	Paula McFetridge
Eileen, *a 22 year-old girl*	Helen Trew

The play takes place in the ground floor flat of an old Victorian terrace house.

NOTE

Iggy's room will be defined by a square of light centre stage. Outside the square of light are five chairs. The actors remain on stage throughout the play. When an actor enters or exits they do so solely in relation to Iggy's room. When not involved in the action (ie, in Iggy's room) the actors sit motionless on their chairs. The only exception to this is Eileen. Her first entrance is from off-stage, after which she follows the same routine as the others. It is important that throughout the play each character treats Iggy's room as their own.

The stage is in darkness but for a spotlight on IGGY, *who is sitting at his desk. He is holding a pencil in front of his face, moving it back and forth like the arm of a metronome. Suddenly he snaps the pencil in half. Lighting goes up on Iggy's room.* BEANPOLE *is lying stoned on the bed, playing with a paper aeroplane. He throws it across the room.*

BEANPOLE: Fly away little children. [*He lights a joint.*] More medication. Is it today or tomorrow? I've to be somewhere tomorrow. Important, heavy importance kid. Choo choo, the big train is coming. People on big choo choo, can't be late. Upright! Respectable! Pillar! [*Pause*] Wanker! Can't come here, no, no, no, not here, that would be a bad idea.

IGGY: Tomorrow? Linda's coming here tomorrow, a visit from the world outside.

BEANPOLE: Tomorrow? Fuck! No tomorrow is hours away.

IGGY: Linda.

[*The action freezes except for* IGGY. LINDA *enters carrying a suitcase.*]

LINDA: Come with me, Iggy. [*Silence*] I won't be back. [*Silence*] Say something. [*Silence*] Goodbye, Iggy. [*Silence.* LINDA *exits.*]

[*Action resumes*]

IGGY: I have nothing to say.

BEANPOLE: Hours away. Tick-tock, tick-tock, choo-choo. Hunky-dory, happy days, good, good, good. Bye, bye. Not my fault, nothing to do with me, do you understand what I'm saying. Shit happens, what do you do?

IGGY: Why's she coming? [*He takes an imaginary photograph of himself.*] Click, click, click.

[BEANPOLE *walks to the sofa and examines it.*]

BEANPOLE: Sweet little baby doll, where'd she go? Lovely ass. Fucky, fucky, fucky. Upstairs in my little love nest. Sounds, sex,

magic. The three of us, me, you and sweet little baby doll—
share the goodies kid, that's me. It's not tomorrow yet. C'mon
let's wake sweet little baby doll.

[BEANPOLE *exits. The stage darkens, a spotlight on* IGGY *flashes on and
off once and we hear the sound of a camera shutter. A loud burst of*
'Lucy in the Sky with Diamonds'.]

LIZZY [*off-stage*]: Turn that friggin rubbish off, ye bloody eejit.

[*Music fades.* IGGY *lights a cigarette.* JIMMY *enters.*]

JIMMY: I have another one for your wee book, Iggy. This is a gem
this one. There's this man and he has no luck and it's doing
his head in. So he thinks to himself, I'll have to find out about
this. So he decides to ask God why he's no luck. So he starts
making his way to God's cave. He's dandering along and he
bumps into this tree—no hold on, that's not right—the tree's
not first. I've got it, it's a wolf. He bumps into this wolf lying on
the ground absolutely knackered because he hasn't eaten in
the last four days. He says to the wolf, no the wolf says to him
'Where you going?' Your man says, 'I've no luck and I'm going
to ask God what the crack is.' The wolf, who can hardly lift his
head says to him, 'Let me know how you get on, it would be
interesting to know what God has to say about that.' On he
goes and this time he meets a tree, it's one of those stories
where everything talks, you know. The trees last leaf falls to the
ground, it's in a bad way. Your man says, 'I have no luck, blah,
blah, blah.' Oh aye and all the other trees have plenty of
leaves, I forgot that. The tree says, 'Let me know how it goes.'
So your man sets off again.

[LINDA *enters squirting a water pistol.* JIMMY *exits.* IGGY *smiles.*]

LINDA: Take that, and that. Alright, alright, Iggy you win, please
Iggy don't, no don't. I give in. I give in. I'll make a deal, you
put the basin down—I'm thinking—and I'll—[*She screams and
acts as if water has been thrown over her.*] Bastard, you're a dead
man. [*She tries to exit but moves as if someone is blocking her way. She
walks backwards towards the bed while firing the water pistol.*] Get
back, I'll show no mercy. [*She falls on the bed and lies as if pinned

down. Still firing the water pistol she laughs. IGGY *pushes everything off his desk.* LINDA *exits.*]

IGGY: Pictures? Photographs? Where's the fucking struggle in that? Point and press, point and press. Instant truth? No. [*He looks at the pile of books in the corner.*] Useless, fucking useless. [*He moves to books and kicks them.*] Action, not thought. [*He lifts an armful of books and throws them offstage.*] No room to move, no room to live. Other men's lives, fuck that. Action. Don't think do. [*Shouts*] Lizzy, Jimmy, Beanpole are you listening, is my family listening—don't watch, act? She's coming to take pictures of us tomorrow. Don't watch, act.

[IGGY *lies on the bed and falls asleep.* LIZZY *and* JIMMY *enter. He sits and reads the paper. She 'fixes' herself in front of the mirror. During the following scene between* LIZZY *and* JIMMY, BEANPOLE *enters. First he searches Iggy's desk, then searches through the coat on the back of Iggy's chair. He takes a ten pound note from Iggy's coat pocket, holds it up to the light, kisses it then exits.*]

LIZZY: What's wrong you're not wasting your time with all the other 'ole lads down at the bookies.

JIMMY: TV's on the blink. I could nip upstairs to your room and watch the racing there.

LIZZY: No.

JIMMY: I'm not going to raid the place. I'm just going to watch the racing.

LIZZY: Look Jimmy, you're not getting into my room and that's it.

JIMMY: Bring the TV down here then.

LIZZY: No, suppose you drop it on the way down the stairs. No.

JIMMY: It's only a TV for Christ sake.

LIZZY: It's my TV and it's staying where it is. Buy one of your own.

JIMMY: What with?

LIZZY: Ask the bookie for a loan, he's plenty of money.

JIMMY: What would I do with a TV, sitting stuck in your room all day watching that crap.

LIZZY: It's better than plastering your wall with dirty posters.

JIMMY: Is that right?

LIZZY: Yes, that's right.

JIMMY: Bitch.

LIZZY: Bastard.

[IGGY *still asleep.* JIMMY *and* LIZZY *remain on stage. Enter* BEANPOLE *and* LINDA. IGGY *is dreaming They all stand over his bed laughing as if they have just heard a joke.* IGGY *wakes into his dream startled. They stroke and caress him, then take him by the hand and lead him to the desk. He sits. During the following scene they crowd round him, their faces close to his—an interrogation.*]

LINDA: You're the new boy.

LIZZY: This is your room.

BEANPOLE: The biggest.

JIMMY: The best.

LIZZY: Has all the furniture.

ALL: Bastard!

LINDA: She swallowed a cabbage whole.

BEANPOLE: He's no eyeballs.

JIMMY: She smokes old socks.

LIZZY: He eats bowls of sago.

ALL: We're interesting people.

BEANPOLE: Escaping from life you no longer want to lead?

JIMMY: Wants to escape from people?

BEANPOLE: We're not real people.

ALL: We're interesting people.

LINDA: What are you?

LIZZY: Yes?

BEANPOLE: Am?

JIMMY: Was?

LINDA: Was.

LIZZY: A journalist!

BEANPOLE: Too many words in the world.

JIMMY: Too many words.

LINDA: Am.

JIMMY: A bookie.

LIZZY: A writer of books.

LINDA: Brave exciting little boy.

BEANPOLE: No starving children left behind?

LIZZY: We don't like starving children left behind.

LINDA: It's safe here.

JIMMY: Are we in the book?

LIZZY: Me?

LINDA: Me?

JIMMY: Me?

BEANPOLE: Me?

LINDA: Brave exciting little boy to leave work and enter into the wilderness.

BEANPOLE: No wife?

LIZZY: No house?

JIMMY: No car?

BEANPOLE: No children?

LIZZY: No job?

LINDA: You're the new boy.

LIZZY: You are.

JIMMY: You are.

LINDA: You are.

BEANPOLE: You are.

> [LIZZY, JIMMY, BEANPOLE *exit.* LINDA *watches* IGGY *sleep then takes a camera from her photography equipment. She takes a few shots of the books Iggy kicked. She moves to* IGGY *taking shots of him at different angles.* 'Smile.' *She scatters his papers round his desk then takes more shots. She nudges him. Just before he fully wakes she takes one last picture.*]

IGGY: Any cigarettes?

LINDA: I've stopped.

IGGY: On the bed.

> [*She hands him one. He lights it and coughs.*]

LINDA: Haven't you given up?

IGGY: Yes.

> [LINDA *hands him a flower.*]

IGGY: Stolen?

LINDA: Of course.

IGGY: You're such a romantic.

LINDA: It looked pretty, it'll brighten the room up. This room always needed brightening up.

IGGY: Did it indeed?

[IGGY *jumps up puts the flower in Linda's mouth and tangoes with her.*]

IGGY: Do you come here often?

LINDA: Only in the mating season.

IGGY [*in French accent*]: My name is Phillipe and I live in a roof top apartment overlooking wet Parisian streets. What is your name?

LINDA: Boris.

[*They laugh.*]

IGGY: You move well Boris, you have danced the tango before.

LINDA: No words, just dance, you savage.

[*They ra, ta ta etc.*]

IGGY: I see you have a camera, Boris.

LINDA: I'm on a mission. I need pictures of a writer and misfits for an exhibition, my first and last exhibition.

[IGGY *stops dancing and poses for her.*]

IGGY: Sorry just misfits today.

[*She puts the flower in his mouth and sits him down in front of the desk.*]

LINDA: Writing, smoking cigarettes, drinking cups of coffee, you know the type of thing. Just pretend I'm not here.

[*She fixes his collar and ruffles his hair. She puts a pencil in his hand and opens a book in front of him. She takes a picture. He removes flower, drops pencil, closes book.*]

IGGY: Wrong pose, it's not the real me. A different pose. I'll tell you a story and you take a photograph of my head, see what's inside it.

LINDA: Why?

IGGY: To capture the truth in focus for ever and a day.

LINDA: It doesn't work like that.

IGGY: Do it anyway, for me, for old times' sake. Put the camera up to your eye, that's better. I forced myself to leave this room last week—first time in months.

LINDA: You should get out more, it's not ...

IGGY: Keep the camera up to your eye, the truth may appear at any moment.

LINDA: Don't push it, Iggy.

IGGY: Just friendly debate—writer photographer stuff, non-contact sport. I'm a writer, an artist, so I did an arty thing I went to the theatre. Arty people should do arty things, don't you think? The play was about a lesbian who had the hots for a straight person and how that was messing her head up—big social issues. Don't click until I say.

LINDA: I choose the moment—it's what I do.

IGGY: I went for a pint, make a night of it you know. The pub was packed, couldn't move, didn't know anyone, didn't meet anyone—to hell with that. I'm sitting on the bus looking out the window, watching the world outside, four seats behind me two fellas are giving the girl opposite a hard time. I keep looking out the window their noise is embarrassing me. "I'd love to fuck you right up the arse, do you hear me, right up the arse." I need to get off the bus, I'm frightened. Some fella steps in, a good guy, a knight in shining armour. Punch, kick, kick, punch—blood. The good guy's in a mess. I listened, I watched, but I didn't move. Take the photograph.

LINDA: No.

IGGY: Take the fucking photograph. [*Pause*] Please. [*She does.*]

[*The stage darkens, a spotlight on* IGGY *flashes on and off once and we hear the sound of a camera shutter.*]

I can't write, I just can't do it, whatever it was isn't there anymore. I ran back here and jotted down a few notes. I could have helped him. I could have made a difference in the real world but I didn't, I just watched, I did what I do. I observed. No use. And now I can't write, the outside world frightens me and I know all there is to know in here.

LINDA: Move in with me, we need to be alone.

[*She sets her camera down and puts her arms around him, her actions quickly move from comforting to passion. She strokes his head. She kisses him. They move to the bed. He pulls her t-shirt off. The action freezes except for* IGGY. JIMMY *enters. He continues with the story he was previously telling. He stands behind* IGGY *talking over his shoulder.*]

JIMMY: He comes across this beautiful house in the middle of the woods, lovely garden, the whole works. There's a girl lives in it on her own and she's an absolute honey. She's crying her lamps out because she's lonely. He tells her the crack, she stops crying and says, 'Let me know what happens,' and he's away on his bike again. He arrives at God's cave. 'Alright Big Man how's it going,' and all that nonsense. 'I've no luck' the man says. God says, 'There's no problem here. Your luck's out there, you just have to grasp the opportunity when it comes along.' So he says his goodbyes and goes to look for his luck.

[JIMMY *exits. Action resumes.* BEANPOLE *enters in his underpants.*]

BEANPOLE: Jesus, sunlight. [*He goes to wardrobe and takes a suit out.*]

LINDA: Is there no privacy in this place, must everything be done in public?

BEANPOLE: Linda baby, lovely jugs, kid.

LINDA: Jesus.

BEANPOLE [*holding suit against himself*]: What do you think?

LINDA: Your timing's shit, that's what I think.

IGGY: Lovely, beautiful, gorgeous.

BEANPOLE [*to* LINDA]: What?

LINDA: You're like de Niro. Close the door behind you.

[IGGY *sits up and lights a cigarette.*]

BEANPOLE [*to* IGGY]: A nice tie?

LINDA [*to* IGGY]: Tell him to leave.

BEANPOLE: Linda kid, Iggy's space is our space.

LINDA: I think I'll call my exhibition 'Pictures of a Fish Bowl'.

IGGY: In that drawer.

BEANPOLE [*holding the tie against himself*]: Respectable?

LINDA: Pictures of a fish bowl.

IGGY: Very respectable.

BEANPOLE: Good. [*He lies on the bed between them.*] Linda!

LINDA: What?

BEANPOLE [*offering her a smoke*]: Do you want a blast of this?

LINDA: No. No Beanpole I don't.

BEANPOLE: I love you kid, you know that, don't you?

LINDA [*smiling*]: You're full of shit. What is it you want?

BEANPOLE: Take a photo of me, now, here. It's important.

IGGY: Fish bowl photography, Linda, it's in demand.

BEANPOLE: Will you, it has to be done now, I've to be somewhere soon?

[LINDA *prepares to take a picture of him.*]

BEANPOLE: No, not that type, this is something else. [*He sets the joint in an ashtray.*] I need the whistle and flute on and I want to sit at Iggy's desk.

[BEANPOLE *continues to dress.* LINDA *is watching him through her camera.* IGGY *lights a cigarette.* JIMMY *enters sits on Iggy's desk and continues with his story.*]

JIMMY: All he can think of is 'the luck's out there, must grasp it, take the opportunity.' The first one he meets is the wee honey. 'How'd it go?' she says. 'Your luck's out there, you just got to grasp the opportunity,' he says. She says, 'Look I've this big house, lovely gardens but I've no one to share it with, plus I'm a good cook and I'm unbelievable in the sack. Do you want to marry me?' Your man says, 'Sorry I've no time for all that. I'm busy looking for my luck. I have to be ready to grasp the opportunity when it comes along.' So after knocking her back he's on his way again. He meets the wolf, no that's wrong. I keep on getting the two of them mixed up, it's the tree next. The tree says to him, 'I'm withering away because all those gold bars lying on my roots are stopping the water from getting through, you wouldn't take the gold bars away.' Your man's the same crack, 'I've no time, looking for my luck, grasp the opportunity, have to go.' Finally he meets the wolf again, who's still starving. 'What did God have to say?' says the wolf.

Your man says to the wolf, 'God says your luck's out there and you jut have to grasp the opportunity when it come along.' So the wolf did.

[IGGY *looks at* JIMMY.]

BEANPOLE [*dressed except for trousers, which he leaves off. To* LINDA]: I need this now, use one of those camera's where it pops out right away. Is the suit me or what?

LINDA: You'll knock them dead.

JIMMY [*to* IGGY]: Don't you get it, the wolf eats him.

BEANPOLE [*to* IGGY]: Comb.

IGGY [*still looking at* JIMMY]: What?

BEANPOLE [*nudging* IGGY]: Comb, have you a comb?

[JIMMY *exits.*]

IGGY: No comb.

LINDA: Here use my brush. What's this for?

BEANPOLE [*at mirror brushing his hair*]: I'm going to frame it and send it to my ma, just in case she's worried about me, you know.

LINDA: A school photograph?

BEANPOLE: Yeah, that's it kid, a school photograph. Tidy the desk up. Turn the lamp on. It's not just right, it needs something else. [*To* IGGY] Have you a brief case?

IGGY: No.

BEANPOLE: Linda?

LINDA: No.

BEANPOLE: Shit. A couple of books that'll do. [*Gets some books. Opens one in front of him, stacks the rest on the desk.*] Right I'm ready, give it your best shot kid.

LINDA: Are you sure, you wouldn't like a make-up job or anything?

BEANPOLE: Blow job?

LINDA: In your dreams.

BEANPOLE: There was a time when—

LINDA: Long gone—Long gone.

BEANPOLE: Touchy kid.

LINDA: Do you want the photograph or not?

BEANPOLE [*pretending to read book.*]: I'm ready.

[*She takes a photograph. He takes jacket off loosens tie, sits on the sofa and lights a joint.*]

BEANPOLE [*handing* IGGY *the joint*]: Some medication?

LINDA [*to* IGGY]: Are you going to get stoned?

IGGY: Just pretend I'm not here you said.

LINDA: That doesn't mean I want to be ignored.

IGGY: I'm not, I'm just doing what I do.

BEANPOLE: [*Relaxing, eyes closed.* LINDA *takes a photo of him.*] Don't let me fall asleep, I've to be somewhere soon.

[IGGY *and* LINDA *sit in silence. She takes the joint off him, has one smoke then puts it out.*]

IGGY: Old times' sake.

LINDA: Do you want to go for a walk?

IGGY: No. You're not very good at this pretending I'm not here business are you?

LINDA: I am normally.

IGGY: What is it then, me, this place or are you just having a shit day?

LINDA: It's you in this place.

IGGY: What are you doing here Linda, when you left you said you weren't coming back, so why are you here?

LIZZY: I miss you.

IGGY: I miss you.

LINDA: Move out.

IGGY: No. Move back.

LINDA: No.

EILEEN [*off-stage*]: Hello! Hello!

BEANPOLE: [*Eyes open*] Shit, I forgot about her.

[*Freeze frame except for* IGGY. EILEEN *enters. She speaks as if engaged in conversation with the people on stage.* IGGY *watches her but remains silent.*]

EILEEN [*to* BEANPOLE]: Hi. Why didn't you wake me? Hoping to make your escape boy before I got up? [*To* LINDA] You there, at the party? It's a big place this, is it a boarding house or something? Do you live here? It must be great crack living here.

Back home I live on a farm—a bit dead, not like this place—no parties or that. I'm staying with friends at the moment, cousins really. I've a job interview tomorrow. I'm only up a few days. Do yous have many parties here? I talk too much don't I, my da's always telling me that, I get it from him. My name's Eileen. I always say what I think, people don't like that sometimes, but it's the way I am. [*To* LINDA] Are you just visiting then? Just dropped in to see what you're missing, I'm a bit like that. When I stay in I always feel I'm missing something but you never are. Is that all your stuff, are you a photographer? If I get this interview I'll be working behind the meat counter in Dunnes. Maybe they'll take a fancy to me and you'll see me on some of their posters. A couple of the lads back home think I'd make a good model, my ears are too big though. What do you think, you must have a good eye for them things. You can get your ears pinned back you know. My brother takes pictures, only of the local football team though. He has them hanging all over the place, wouldn't take one of me though. Pictures of strangers everywhere but wouldn't take one of his own sister, funny that. [*To* IGGY] What do you do?

[*Action resumes.* BEANPOLE *smokes a joint and indicates to* EILEEN *to sit on his knee. She does.* LINDA *looks at* EILEEN *through a camera but doesn't take a picture.*]

LINDA: He's a writer.

EILEEN [*to* IGGY]: Books? I don't—

LINDA: Book. A book.

EILEEN: I don't read much myself. I'll read yours though 'cause I know you now. Maybe you wouldn't want me to read it though, people can be precious about things like that, can't they?

LINDA: It's not finished.

EILEEN: Has it a title yet? People always go by titles don't they, if you've a good title sure that's have the battle. What is it, what's yours.

[BEANPOLE *sporadically burst into laughter from now until he exists. This gives* EILEEN *the giggles.*]

IGGY: It's not important.

EILEEN: Tells us.

IGGY [*waits for* LINDA *to answer*]: *Deafening Falls.* Apparently the people who live near Niagara Falls can't hear the noise of them anymore, because they're so used to it.

EILEEN: I don't like the title. You don't mind me saying that do you? Where's Niagara Falls? Canada? I've never been there—I've never been anywhere—it must be beautiful. What's it like?

IGGY: I haven't been there. I don't know.

EILEEN: What's it about? Everybody wants to write a book don't they but they never do. Why'd you start, did you have a good story is that it?

IGGY: I thought I'd find out the truth.

[*The action freezes. The stage darkens but for a spotlight on* IGGY *which flashes on and off once and we hear the sound of a camera shutter.*]

IGGY: I always felt that writing a book would somehow make a difference. I didn't have a story in my head but I thought if I could put down on paper what other people thought it might help me understand things, and if they read it then they'd understand things and I'd be fucking immortal.

[*Action resumes.*]

EILEEN: Would you not be better writing a comedy, a wee bit of crack.

[IGGY *ignores her.*]

BEANPOLE: Have a blast. [*Hands her a joint he's been smoking.*]

EILEEN: Yous certainly know how to enjoy yourselves. I never took any of this stuff until yesterday.

LINDA: Eileen put the joint in your mouth. Now blow the smoke up, that's it. [*She takes a photograph.*]

EILEEN: Dunnes will hardly want that one.

[BEANPOLE *whispers to* EILEEN. *They continue whispering and giggling for some time.* LINDA *takes a photograph of the two of them.* JIMMY *enters. His suit is old but neat. He is wearing a pair of trainers.*]

JIMMY: Friggin' dogshit everywhere, it's like tiptoeing through a bloody minefield. Dogshit everywhere and they're handing out leaflets about 'Putting the Smile Back into Belfast' and some bloody fireworks display.

LINDA: That's tonight, the paper's sending me to cover it. [*To* IGGY] Why don't you go with me, you might enjoy it, get you out for a while.

IGGY: I don't want to go out.

JIMMY: They'd be better cleaning the bloody streets instead of letting squibs off.

EILEEN [*the dope taking effect*]: Bang, fizz, fizz, bang. Having fun boys and girls? [*Back to the whispering and giggling.*]

JIMMY [*about* EILEEN]: One of the music man's friends. [*He sits, takes his shoes off and rubs his feet.*] Bloody feet. Alright Linda luv, how's things?

LINDA [*taking a photograph of* JIMMY]: Couldn't be better, Jimmy.

JIMMY: Aye, spend you life behind a bar and you end up with feet like bloody 'ole baps. Iggy, guess who I ran into? Nigel, do you remember him?

IGGY: No.

BEANPOLE: You wouldn't, he had this room before you did.

IGGY: What was he like?

BEANPOLE: He was some guy lived here—I don't know. What do you mean what was he like, he lived here kid? What?

IGGY: Was he a private person, did he keep that door locked? What was he like?

BEANPOLE: Iggy kid, what is that, did he lock the door? What?

IGGY: Jimmy, did he keep the door locked or did everyone just pop in and out whenever it suited them?

LINDA: Iggy, what is the problem?

IGGY: The question is simple enough did he keep the fucking door locked or didn't he?

EILEEN: Lock up the doors. Up fuck the doors.

IGGY: Forget it.

JIMMY: That door's never been able to lock properly.

IGGY: Thank you.

JIMMY: Nigel, he graduated today. I was walking by it all, spotted him and went over. Some pomp around the university today. [EILEEN *jumps up and waltzes around the room, then stands on* IGGY*'s desk. Slowly she removes her t-shirt. She beckons* BEANPOLE *with her finger.*]

EILEEN: Fireworks, bang, fizz, bang—explode. Big fucking explosions. [*To* BEANPOLE.] Can you dance boy, are you a good mover are you?

BEANPOLE [*stopping her*]: Relax kid, relax.

EILEEN: Dance. [*Arms outstretched, she twirls.*] I'm a good mover boy, when I'm allowed to be. Dance. Can you do the fandango, boy?

JIMMY: That Nigel's a right fella you know.

BEANPOLE [*breaking away*]: I told you. I have to go kid. I've to be somewhere else, it's important.

EILEEN: [*Gets down off table*] Stay and dance with me. [*She grabs his crotch.*] Rocket man! Fireworks Boy!

[BEANPOLE *begins to exit then turns back and takes* EILEEN *by the hand.*]

EILEEN: My hero. [*She kisses him.*] Show me your record collection. On your back, carry me on your back. [*She jumps on his back.*] Take a picture, quick a picture.

[LINDA *doesn't move.* EILEEN *and* BEANPOLE *exit.*]

EILEEN [*off-stage*]: Bang, bang, fizz, fizz, pop.

JIMMY: He's some operator isn't he? I used to put it about myself a bit, oh aye. Jimmy the bull that was me. [*Silence*] The graduation was some crack. I met Nigel's parents, lovely people. Strawberries and cream and an 'ole yarn.

[IGGY *and* LINDA *ignore what* JIMMY *is saying during the following.* LINDA *sits on the floor in front of* IGGY*'s desk. She is playing with her camera as if it were a toy.*]

JIMMY: They have a lot to be proud off in that boy, yes indeed fine stock.

IGGY: Why didn't you take the photograph of her?

LINDA: Eileen's me a few years ago, isn't she?

JIMMY: I got my picture taken with them. There's one of me and Nigel and then there's one of the four of us.

IGGY: Is she?

LINDA: This place, it does that when your first come here, draws you
     in. You feel carefree, cocooned from the world, nothing but
     good times ahead.

IGGY: She's just passing through, Linda.

JIMMY: Nigel's da was telling me he's just bought a wee pub,
     something with a bit of class about it I'm sure.

LINDA: This is a dangerous place Iggy, everyone thinks they're just
     passing through, there's something better just around the
     corner and then without knowing it they're stuck here, forever.
     Why can't you see that?

IGGY: Is that why you left?

JIMMY: I asked Nigel to put a word in for me, for a wee part-time job.
     I told him to come round tonight, we'd have a wee bit of a party
     for him, celebrate his graduation you know. He said he'd let me
     know then about the job.

IGGY: Is it?

LINDA: It's seedy Iggy, it's a dim, grubby, bleak place, there's no
     heroes live here.

IGGY: No, but that's OK, heroes only fuck things up for the rest of
     us.

JIMMY: What do you think about that? A wee part-time job Iggy,
     what do you think?

IGGY: [*to* JIMMY]: What?

JIMMY: The party I'm throwing for Nigel tonight, he's going to tell
     me if I've got a part-time job in his da's new pub.

IGGY: [*not interested*]: That's good.

JIMMY: I think I'll nip down to the bookies and do a wee bet for
     Nigel, celebrate his graduation. Maybe bring me a bit of luck
     with the job.

     [JIMMY *exits. Suddenly 'Lucy in the Sky with Diamonds' by the Beatles
     blurts out. The noise is from Beanpole's room.* IGGY *sits at his desk.*
     LINDA *moves some furniture. She is getting the room the way she wants
     it.*]

LIZZY [*off-stage*]: Turn the bloody thing off. [LINDA *hands* IGGY *a cup
     then prepares to take a picture of him.*]

LINDA: Take a drink.

IGGY: There's nothing in it.

LINDA: Pretend.

[IGGY *pretends to drink. She takes a photograph of him.*]

LINDA: Write something down.

IGGY: No. [LIZZY *enters. She wears a black dressing gown trimmed with fake fur.*]

LIZZY: Has he somebody in his room? I'll put a hammer through that record player, I swear I will. You can't hear your own bloody TV with all that racket.

LINDA: Just stand the way you are, Lizzy—just like that.

LIZZY: What are you doing?

LINDA: I'm going to take a picture.

LIZZY: No chance, I'm like a gyp. When I'm all dolled up, not now.

LINDA: But that's what I want.

LIZZY: What? A photograph of me like a gyp.

LINDA: I want it to look natural.

LIZZY: I look more natural with my make-up on. [*She goes to the mirror and 'tidies' herself up.*] Cover the cracks up. [*She examines her face.*] Did I ever tell you Iggy I used to be a singer?

IGGY: No.

LIZZY: Nothing glamorous, just round the clubs and that. [*Sings*] "When Frankie and Johnny were lovers." That was my man's name, Frankie. He never knew a thing about it. He was a sailor—when he was away I did the clubs. When he was at home me and him sat in the house. Sure it never works out the way you want it to, isn't that the way things are?

IGGY: You had a secret life?

[*Action freezes except for* IGGY. *He walks around* LIZZY, *looking her up and down, examining her.* "You had a secret life, a singer." *He walks back to his desk and sits down.* "A singer." LIZZY *sings two verses of 'Hey Big Spender'. Her performance is crude and vulgar, her physical movements are openly sexual Her voice is loud and harsh, she is practically shouting. After the song is finished, she freezes again,* IGGY *stares at her.* "You had a secret life, brilliant." *Action resumes.*]

LIZZY: We all have our moments, Iggy. [*She moves centre stage.*] The picture, I'm ready.

LINDA: Lizzy they're for any exhibition, not the mantelpiece.

LIZZY: They're all pictures, aren't they? People just look at them, don't they? Well, if it's going to be of me I want them to see me half decent. Take one of me and Iggy. People'll think he's my toyboy. Here comb your hair.

IGGY: Tell me more about the secret life.

LIZZY: Comb your hair.

[IGGY *combs his hair.* LIZZY *sits on his knee.*]

LIZZY: That's better. Smile. [LINDA *takes a photograph.*] And another one. [LIZZY *puts her arms around* IGGY*'s neck and pushes her face against his.*] You need your hair washed. What do you think Linda, doesn't he need his hair washed?

LINDA: Probably.

LIZZY: If I had money, Iggy, me and you could be away somewhere.

[LINDA *takes photographs of* LIZZY *during this scene.*]

LIZZY: Somewhere tropical. A big white house on the edge of the beach. During the day we'd just soak up the sun, have a few drinks by the pool, maybe take a walk into the village, buy something fresh to eat. [*She gets off his knee and becomes animated, involved.*] At night we'd stroll down to the beach. I've a long white gown on and you in a dinner suit. We'd walk along the beach barefoot. There's a party on the beach, everyone's looking at us. [*She starts to twirl, losing herself in her thoughts.*] The soft beat of the drums, a warm breeze touching your face. The waves and the beat of the drum. And we'd dance, oh how we would dance. [*She twirls faster.*] And dance, and dance. [*She stops suddenly in front of* IGGY.] What do you think toyboy, is that for you?

[*During the next brief scene* IGGY *ignores both* LINDA *and* LIZZY. *At the same time* LINDA *ignores* LIZZY. IGGY *sits at his desk, gathers his papers and jots something down.*]

LINDA: Did I tell you I bought a new car, well second-hand, a Renault. It was either a car or a holiday.

LIZZY: I've never been outside Ireland—do you know that?

LINDA: I thought the car would be more useful. I can always go on holiday next year, might even take the car with me, not camping though. I couldn't be bothered with that anymore.

LIZZY: My Frankie always said he'd take me away somewhere but he never did.

LINDA: I want a bit of comfort now, a nice hotel, someone to pamper me.

LIZZY: When he was away on the ships he'd send me a postcard though. I've postcards from every corner of the world and I've been nowhere. He saw some beautiful places my Frankie did. I have them all upstairs in a box. I've always meant to put them in a book, they might even be worth something now.

[IGGY *turns suddenly and addresses* LIZZY.]

IGGY: Have you posters or anything like that from your singing days? I'd love to see them, anything at all, old newspaper clippings, anything.

LIZZY: I told you my Frankie knew nothing about it—why would I want to keep anything, he might've found them mightn't he, and that would have spoiled everything. I'm away for a shower.

[EILEEN *enters wearing only* BEANPOLE'*s t-shirt.*]

EILEEN [*singing*]: "Lucy in the sky with diamonds." Rocket man forgot his skins. [*She lifts the cigarette papers and exits singing.*] "Picture yourself in a boat on the river."

LIZZY [*laughing*]: Rocket man, Jesus Christ.

[LIZZY *exits.*]

IGGY: Do you realise what happened there? Did you see it, were you listening?

LINDA: I've to go Iggy, some new business enterprise centre opening up, my boss wants some pictures of it, God only knows why.

IGGY: You should get yourself a car, save you all that taxiing about. Listen to me, you don't listen to me, that thing about Lizzy being a singer, why'd she tell me that, and why now, why today?

LINDA: I don't know, she was just making small talk.

IGGY: There's more to it than that. This was her secret life, the one thing truly hers, and she let it out just like that. It's like sometimes things just happen and you don't know why, but you know they're right.

LINDA: All she did was tell you she sang in clubs and didn't tell her husband, she didn't explain the secret of life.

IGGY: It was the secret of her life. Look, I'm a writer and I can't make myself write, something's wrong and I don't know what it is. I watch things but I just can't seem to get behind them. And then Lizzy just pops up and there's the truth right in front of me—a person struggling to do something, hoping they're going to get there but it's never going to happen. I saw how things really are. If you had taken a photograph of her at that very moment you wouldn't have got it, you wouldn't have got behind the image, you wouldn't have got the truth.

LINDA: The photograph would have shown her as she is, as she really is, now.

IGGY: The picture would have been incomplete, that's what I'm saying, you're not listening to me, it would have been on the surface, no depth, two dimensional.

LINDA: Everything we create is incomplete. Why waste your time struggling for a truth that isn't there? You have a look and capture what you can that's all. You just do it for Christ sake Iggy, it doesn't have to be angst ridden all the time, you just do it. The struggle's not out there, it's in you—why can't you see that?

IGGY: I'm not wasting my time struggling for a truth that isn't there. It's important, we all need to know how things really are—the truth, I have to focus on that, see it, say it. [*Silence*] I miss this about us. Remember we used to sit up night after night smoking our brains out and talking about what we did. How we tried to express ourselves and how that was going to make a difference in the world.

LINDA: I don't miss it, Iggy. I did all the talking I had to, it's time to get on with things, be who you are, do what you do, accept it. We're not going to change the world, we never were.

IGGY: That's sad.

LINDA: You wanted the truth.

[LINDA *gathers up her equipment. They stand in silence.*]

IGGY: We've been here before.

[LINDA *exits.* IGGY *sits on the bed. He gets up and paces the room.*]

IGGY: Hey big spender, spend a little time with me.

[IGGY *imitates* LIZZY *singing 'Hey Big Spender'.* EILEEN *bursts in.* IGGY *stops.*]

EILEEN: What's keeping you, Beanpole boy?

IGGY: Not here.

EILEEN: Doesn't hang around much, keeps himself busy, doesn't he?

IGGY: Not normally.

EILEEN: Do you always do that?

IGGY: What?

EILEEN: Answer things that aren't really questions? Can I wait here for him?

IGGY: Feel free.

[*Silence*]

EILEEN: It's a great place you have here, full of crack.

IGGY: I have? I don't own it, I just rent a room like the rest of them.

EILEEN: I thought you were the landlord. The way everyone uses the room I thought you were the landlord.

IGGY: They have nowhere else to go.

EILEEN: Where do you go then? Do you disappear into your book or something, do you?

IGGY: No, I don't disappear into anything? I live here just like the rest of them.

EILEEN: People lose themselves in their work, don't they? I thought maybe that's what you did when you do your writing. It's not a crime, I only thought ...

IGGY: Why? Are you interested, in my work that is?

EILEEN: Not really. I'm only passing the time, making conversation. Sure you don't care whether I'm interested in it or not anyway.

You treat me like I don't understand anything so why would you be interested in what I think of your book. If it was on sale you wouldn't want me to buy it, sure you wouldn't?

IGGY: Of course I would.

EILEEN: Liar. You don't think I'd understand it, so reading it would be a waste of time. When people write books and that, they do it for people, don't they, it's like they're aiming what they say at people. Well it's my guess that book of yours isn't aimed at me.

IGGY: What makes you think I treat you like you don't understand anything?

EILEEN: Don't you?

IGGY: No.

EILEEN: When I first came in you ignored me. I was talking nine to the dozen, you could have said something but you didn't. Then when I asked you about your book you wouldn't answer, as if it was something the rest of us shouldn't know about.

IGGY: I was watching you that's all.

EILEEN: I know, you made the whole thing awkward, that's why I was talking so much.

IGGY: The other two, Beanpole and Linda they—

EILEEN: They were listening, you were just watching.

IGGY: I thought they were ignoring you. Beanpole didn't really want you there so he ignored you, thinking you'd go away.

EILEEN: That's not true, he asked me to stay, he asked me to stay didn't he.

IGGY: I didn't hear him.

EILEEN: Well he did, I heard, he said it. You were too bloody busy looking at me to hear what anyone was saying. He said it.

IGGY: OK he said it. [*Pause*] Do you mind if I ask you something, a question?

EILEEN: When we were kids, me and my brother used to play a game called questions. I'd ask him a question and he'd give me two answers. One the truth and one lies, you had to find out which was which. Do you want to play?

IGGY: OK. What are you doing here?

EILEEN: That one's no good, it has to be something you don't know the answer to, you know what I'm doing here, waiting on Beanpole.

IGGY: No, that's not the question. I mean what are you doing in this place, haven't you somewhere else to be—something else to do.

EILEEN: If you didn't want me to wait here why didn't you say, I'll go upstairs to wait, it doesn't bother me, I thought it would be a bit of company for you that's all.

IGGY: I don't mean you can't wait here, that's not what I meant.

EILEEN: Somewhere else to be, something else to do, you think my life doesn't mean anything don't you.

IGGY: What?

EILEEN: You do, don't you?

IGGY: Don't be ridiculous.

EILEEN: I'm not ridiculous and I'm not stupid. I understand plenty. As if I had nothing else to do but hang around here and waste my time. Well you're wrong. I've a job interview tomorrow—I know it's only Dunnes, nothing really important like being a writer—well until the interview I'm just having a bit of crack that's all. I'm here because I want to be here, but that doesn't suit you, sure it doesn't. There has to be a darker side to it or something. Well there's not, a bit of crack that's all. I could be somewhere else if I wanted to be but I don't, do you understand that, are you listening or are you just watching me again?

IGGY: I just wanted to know if—

EILEEN: Oh, I know what you wanted to know alright—you wanted to know if I've a seedy past—you wanted to know if I've been raped or if my da abused me, or maybe he's a drunk and my ma's run away with someone—you want to know the reasons why I'm escaping don't you—well I'm sorry to disappoint you but there's none. I'm up here for a job and that's it.

IGGY: I wasn't trying to ... I didn't think you ... Look all I was doing was making conversation, the same as you. I asked a question, one question that's all. I'll tell you what, forget I asked you anything. We'll start again, OK?

EILEEN: No.

[EILEEN *exits.* IGGY *sits on the edge of his bed.*]

IGGY: I just wanted to know if she was going to stay here, that's all. I don't understand that, what happened there, did I do something wrong, what? [*He moves and sits at his desk.*] Ignored her? She thought I ignored her, Jesus!

[BEANPOLE *enters. He stands in front of the mirror and examines himself. He takes a photograph from his pocket and looks at it, then stares at the mirror. He spits on his reflection.* EILEEN *enters, still in* BEANPOLE*'s t-shirt. She is humming a tune and dancing.*]

EILEEN: Beanpole, party time, Beanpole. [*She moves close to him and rubs her body against him.*] Miss me?

BEANPOLE: Don't.

[EILEEN *moves away from him. During the following conversation she hums and dances on the spot. She is listening to him and no more.*]

EILEEN: I like your hair in a ponytail, it suits you.

BEANPOLE: I need it cut, short, respectable.

EILEEN: It wouldn't be you then though would it?

BEANPOLE: Me? [*He tosses her the photograph.*] Who's that, me? Is that me?

EILEEN: It's you alright, smartened up a bit but it's you. You look like a trendy teacher in it, my geography teacher was a bit ...

BEANPOLE: [*Snatches the photograph from her and rips it up.*] That's a fucking fool that's who that is. [*He stares at* EILEEN.]

EILEEN: What?

BEANPOLE: What age are you?

EILEEN: Twenty-two. I'll be twenty-three in three months' time.

BEANPOLE: I've two daughters about your age, they live in Dublin with their mother.

EILEEN: You're about my da's age then. So what, is that what's bothering you?

BEANPOLE: I haven't seen them for a while. I was meant to meet them today. The suit, a couple of respectable photographs, impress them, show them what a great fella their da is. I didn't go. I saw the two of them standing outside the book shop, that was my idea, outside a book shop, as if it was a place I knew well. I just stood there and looked, half an hour maybe more, then they left.

[EILEEN *is bored. Uninterested in what* BEANPOLE *is saying, she lies on the sofa and inspects her feet.*]

BEANPOLE: Look at me for Christ sake, hair down round my arse and a suit that isn't my own. [IGGY *wakes up and lights a cigarette.*] I was going to tell them I was a journalist. Jesus. Do you know what I do for a living, how I earn my keep? I sell dope. On Wednesday I buy a big chunk of dope and on Thursday I break it up and sell it. I'm 44 years of fucking age and I sell blow, that's it, that's what I've ended up with. How do you tell your kids that—I'm meant to be someone to them, I'm meant to have done something with my life. You know what I've achieved in 44 years, the only thing? I can juggle. I taught myself to juggle. [*He lifts whatever three objects are near to him and juggles.*] I'm good, aren't I? I should have juggled in front of my kids and pretended I was a fucking street artist. [*He stops suddenly, letting two of the objects hit the floor, the third he looks at and then smashes against the wardrobe.* JIMMY *enters. He is carrying two boxes. One contains bottles of drink, the other fireworks.*]

JIMMY: It touched, the bet touched, "We're in the money, I'm in the money, Nigel's in the money." [*He sets boxes down.*] Drink and fireworks there's going to be some party here tonight.

EILEEN [*becoming alive again*]: Can we light the fireworks now? Lets do it now, lets light them now.

JIMMY: Such a day, bets, graduation, jobs.

[JIMMY *twirls* BEANPOLE *round and then waves the money in front of* IGGY. EILEEN *is at the box with the fireworks in it, as earlier, she is making fireworks noises.*]

EILEEN: Indoor ones?

JIMMY: Such a feeling, a few quid in your pocket and the world's a better place, you know. It gives you that feeling of being

someone, of standing up on your own—the luck's with you.
And then a job on top of that, Jesus what a day.

[JIMMY *takes his jacket off. He is wearing metal armbands, the type a
barman used to wear.*] What do you think, what do you think of
those, do you like them, you got to look the part don't you.

EILEEN: [*To* JIMMY. *Fireworks in her hand*] Please, please, please,
please, please.

JIMMY: Only a few, I want to keep the rest for when Nigel gets here.

EILEEN: [*To* BEANPOLE. *He ignores her and moves to* IGGY.] C'mon rocket
man, a rocket for rocket man.

[EILEEN *and* JIMMY *light a few fireworks and dance round them.*]

BEANPOLE: Do you think I should get my hair cut, kid? Change my
appearance a bit, what do you think?

IGGY: Why are you asking me?

BEANPOLE: Yes or no?

IGGY: Linda thinks Eileen is going to stay here—get caught here,
become a misfit.

BEANPOLE: She's a nice kid.

IGGY: Then tell her to go.

BEANPOLE: If I do that Iggy kid, I'm admitting my life's a piece of
shit.

IGGY: Maybe that's the truth.

BEANPOLE: Fuck you. [*He moves to where* EILEEN *and* JIMMY *are.* JIMMY
moves to where IGGY *is.*]

JIMMY: [*About* EILEEN *and* BEANPOLE] Kids! [*He starts taking bottles of
drink out of the box. He wipes each bottle clean. He takes some glasses
from the box and also wipes them clean.*] New glasses. [*He pours two
drinks, takes one himself and hands the other to* IGGY.] Do you know
what makes a good barman?

[*For the next few minutes* JIMMY *is back where he belongs, behind a bar.*]
Pulling a good pint, having a good memory and knowing when
to talk and when to listen. Whenever I worked in McEntees, a
lovely wee pub it was, it must be ten years ago now, there wasn't
one punter that crossed the door that I didn't know what their
tipple was. [*He adjusts his arm bands.*] A bit tight. I knew

everything about them too, used to come in especially to see me. Oh aye, not many barmen can say that. I had that place like a pin too. Always keep a pub clean, that's another one, good pint, good memory, talk, listen and keep the place gleaming. Most people have to learn them things, with me it was just natural, you never loose something like that. Nigel's da's pub will be a changed place when I get there, I'll show these young bucks a thing or two.

IGGY: Jimmy stop it, he's not coming, there isn't going to be any job.

JIMMY: Why would you say that? I don't understand you saying that.

IGGY: Because it's the truth that's why.

JIMMY: Seeing Linda again upsets you, so you want to ruin my day as well is that it? That's a dirty trick, Iggy, a dirty trick.

IGGY: Linda has nothing to do with this, you're expecting something that's not going to happen. I don't like that, it's sad. Why not face the truth.

JIMMY: Nigel will be here, he won't let me down. You don't even know him, he's a fine upstanding person, an engineer, someone who gets things done in the world, it's a pity you weren't like that. Making stories up about people you don't know that's no way for a young fella to be Iggy. Sad? There's nothing sad about me boy, nothing. I've lived a life alright.

[*Action freezes except for* IGGY. *He is in a state of frustration. He tries to say something to* BEANPOLE *and* EILEEN *but can't. He tries to say something to* JIMMY *but can't. He shouts* "Fuck it. Fuck it." *He stares at the characters on stage and then lies on the sofa.* LINDA *enters, she starts setting up her photography equipment, camera, tripod etc. The action resumes.* LIZZY *enters carrying a tablecloth. During the following brief episode between* IGGY *and* LINDA, *the other characters on stage get the room ready for the party.* JIMMY *sets up a bar, the others tidy the place up, fixing Iggy's books etc. Once the room is ready they start drinking.* JIMMY *is the barman.* BEANPOLE *and* EILEEN *dance with each other. They do not speak at any time during this.*]

LINDA: The first day I arrived here they had a party, much the same

as this one, more exciting though or maybe it just seems that
way now. Has Eileen said she's staying yet?

IGGY: She won't. I told you she's just someone passing through.

LINDA: Move over beside the bed. I need to check the light. She
will.

IGGY: Why are you so sure?

LINDA: She's young, she thinks this place is cool or classic or
awesome or whatever the new word is. That makes the world
outside boring, why wouldn't you stay.

IGGY: Maybe the world outside is boring or violent or disappointing
or lonely.

LINDA: It is Iggy but it's the same here too. I wish you could see that.

IGGY: I see well enough.

LINDA: You don't. If you stay here you'll end up another Beanpole
or Jimmy. You'll take their place. Eileen will take my place then
she'll take Lizzy's. Sit on the edge of the bed. Stand up. Sit down
again.

IGGY: Whenever I first told you I had given up my job, that I had
escaped, I had broken free you admired that. It was like I had
the ability to do that while others didn't.

LINDA: Do it again then, break free from here. I'll talk to someone
at the paper, maybe get you a couple of freelance jobs, get you
back into the way of things, it'll help you see things clearly,
believe me. Move back over beside the bed.

IGGY: That's what you do, isn't it? Move people, arrange them so
they fit into your picture, into your image of how you want
things to be. Move beside the bed, sit on the chair, stand on
your head, change your meaningless life. But you don't ever
listen. I had what you now want and I don't want it back. This
isn't another photo session, Linda. I'm not an image, this is the
real me, I'll be like this no matter where I go. That's the truth.

[*A spotlight on* IGGY *flashes on and off once and we hear the sound of
a camera shutter. Silence.* LINDA *takes a photograph of him. The party
now takes over.* JIMMY *and* LIZZY *are drunk.* BEANPOLE *is stoned and*
EILEEN *is somewhere in between.*]

LIZZY [*to* BEANPOLE]: Song, song.

[BEANPOLE *takes a drink ftom a bottle of whiskey and stands on the bed ready to perform.*]

IGGY [*to* LINDA]: Party time.

BEANPOLE [*singing*]: "La, laa, la la la laaa ... We're busy doing nothing, working the whole day through ... "

[LIZZY *and* JIMMY *waltz around the room, la, la, las etc.* EILEEN *claps in tune.* IGGY *and* LINDA *look at each other.* IGGY *breaks gaze, jumps on bed and begins to sing.* LIZZY *and* JIMMY *coax* LINDA *to dance with them— she forces herself.*]

JIMMY [*singing*]: "Trying to find lots of things not to do. We're busy going nowhere. Isn't it just a crime? We'd like to be unhappy but we never do have the time."

ALL [*except* LINDA]: "We'd like to be unhappy but we never do have the time ... la, la la las ... "

[*The singing stops but the dancing continues as does the la la la.* LINDA *takes photographs of them.* LIZZY *and* EILEEN *are dancing around* JIMMY. *They move closer to him, stroking his head rubbing themselves against him.* LINDA *takes a picture of them.*]

LIZZY [*out of breath*]: A wee picture for Jimmy. Would you like a wee sexy photograph for your wall, Jimmy, to go along with all those books you have?

EILEEN [*rubbing her legs against Jimmy's*]: Do you like the oul girlie photos, Jimmy?

[*They both kiss him on the cheek. He puts his arm around both of them and briefly they dance in a circle.* EILEEN *breaks away.*]

EILEEN: What way would you like us to pose, Jimmy?

[IGGY *and* BEANPOLE *are still dancing and la la la on the bed.*]

LIZZY: It's all tits and bum isn't it, Jimmy ?

[JIMMY *nods.*]

EILEEN: Yes, tits and bum.

[*They look at each other. Quickly* EILEEN *pulls the front of her jumper up and* LIZZY *turns, bends and pulls up the back of her dress.* LINDA *takes a photograph.*]

JIMMY: More, more.

[EILEEN *and* LIZZY *laugh. They strike the same pose as before only the roles are reversed.* LINDA *takes another photograph.* EILEEN *and* LIZZY *stand on as if receiving applause and then curtsey.* JIMMY *unbuttons his shirt and strikes a pose for* LINDA, IGGY *and* BEANPOLE *are still dancing on the bed.*]

LIZZY: More, more.

[*They all laugh.* JIMMY *gives* LIZZY *and* EILEEN *a cigar each. They stand, arm in arm, cigars in mouths posing for* LINDA. *She kneels in front of them taking shots from different angles.*]

LINDA: Brilliant, I love it. Lift your legs up, so Jimmy can hold on to them.

[IGGY *stops dancing.*]

IGGY: More songs, no photographs, more songs.

BEANPOLE: We are the singing people.

IGGY: Frankie and Johnnie—Go.

LINDA: Iggy.

IGGY [*to* LINDA]: Words not pictures. [*To* LIZZY] Connie Francis then? [*Sings*] "Who's sorry now, who's heart is breaking ... " [*Stops*] Not like that one?

[LIZZY *begins to laugh. She centres on* IGGY, *her laughter borders on the uncontrollable.*]

LIZZY: Belfast's answer to Shirley Bassey. [*Still laughing*]

IGGY: What, what is it?

LIZZY: It's you—you're such a fucking eejit, do you know that? You sit here day after day ripping your hair out trying to scribble words down and you think you know it all. [*She laughs*] Night-club singer, that was a lie, do you understand, a wee lie and you fell for it. Just in case you were thinking about putting something about me in your wee book, I thought I'd glitz it up a wee bit. A night-club singer, for fuck sake Iggy get a grip. [*She laughs. They all laugh except for* IGGY.]

LINDA: Photograph on the bed.

[*They get on the bed, all shuffle for position then smile.*]

LINDA: Last one, the session is complete, this is the last one.

[*The action freezes except for* IGGY, *who is sitting at his desk.* IGGY *lights a cigarette and looks at the others on stage. He cleans everything off his desk except for a single blank page. He begins to write. Pause.* IGGY *stops writing. As at the beginning of the play he sits holding a pencil in front of his face moving it back and forth. Suddenly he snaps the pencil in half. The stage lights flash on and off once and we hear the sound of a camera shutter.*]

OTHER DRAMA TITLES

from

LAGAN PRESS

Joseph Tomelty
All Souls' Night & Other Plays
edited and introduced by Damian Smyth
ISBN: 1 873687 04 4
216 pp, £4.95 pbk

Best know as a stage and film actor and as the creator of *The McCooeys*—Northern Ireland's 1940s radio soap which made him a household name in his native place—Joseph Tomelty was also a novelist, short-story writer and, above all, a playwright.

This book, selected by the critic Damian Smyth, gathers for the first time into one volume four major Tomelty plays—the sombre and deeply sad *All Souls' Night* (1948), the lyric *The Singing Bird* (1948), the serio-comic *April in Assagh* (1953) and the controversial *The End House* (1944).

All Souls' Night, set in a dark, passionless world on the east coast of Ulster, is his most critically-acclaimed play. Dealing with poverty, meanness of soul and a mother's consuming greed, it has been described as the best play written in the north of Ireland. It is counterpointed by *April in Assagh*, a play set in a fantastical townland, which is funny and satirical with a dark core of foreboding and published here for the first time. *The End House* creates a Belfast of urban violence after the model of O'Casey. *The Singing Bird*, written for radio in 1948 and later adapted for television, starring Tomelty himself, is a beautiful, pastoral tale of 'a gentle madness'.

Together, these plays provide an indispensable insight into the workings of the double-sided imagination of Tomelty's place— one the one hand deeply obsessive and corrosive, on the other witty, meditative and happy and all with an exhilarating muscular lyricism.

Jennifer Johnston
Three Monologues
Twinkletoes • *Mustn't Forget High Noon* • *Christine*
ISBN: 1 873687 70 2
72 pp, £4.95 pbk

Collected for the first time in print, these monologues represent one of the many dimensions of the talent of Jennifer Johnston, one of Ireland's most important writers since the war.

Revolving round the griefs and traumas caused by the troubles in the north of Ireland, they are an exploration of individual survivals in the midst of the disintegration of life and lives.

Twinkletoes is the story of Karen, a top IRA prisoner's wife; looked up to by her community, she cannot express her loneliness. *Mustn't Forget High Noon* introduces Billy Maltseed, a border Protestant, who has just lost his best friend, a UDR part-timer, shot by the IRA. In *Christine,* Billy's southern Irish wife mourns his death by violence which leaves her alone and childless in a community riven by suspicion.

These monologues—by turns comic and intensely moving— together reclaim the individual voice in the teeth of stereotypes, express most vividly the human beneath the inhuman and the headlines.

Martin Lynch
Three Plays

Dockers • *The Interrogation of Ambrose Fogarty* • *Pictures of Tomorrow*
edited and introduced by Damian Smyth
ISBN: 1 873687 60 5
224 pp, £4.95 pbk

Martin Lynch has been a significant figure in Irish drama since the late 1970s when *They are Taking Down the Barricades* gave expression to contemporary Belfast working-class life. Rooted among the political and imaginative forces bearing upon and emerging from both northern communities, Lynch explored those forces with humour, anger and compassion.

Having committed himself to the values of community-based drama, he wrote a string of popular successes throughout the 1980s. Marked by an accurate ear for dialogue and a pungent wit, the plays chalked out a territory securely his own. Out of this commitment have come also three of the most important plays in the last twenty-five years from the north of Ireland—*Dockers, The Interrogation of Ambrose Fogarty* and *Pictures of Tomorrow*.

Dockers is a boisterous recreation of working-class life in Belfast's famed Sailortown district. Reminiscent of Dario Fo but rigorously rooted in the sadness of real political conflict, *The Interrogation of Ambrose Fogarty* is a most vivid, pointed and funny play dealing with the ironies and absurdities of police detention. With *Pictures of Tomorrow*, Lynch attempts to deal with the disillusion of left-wing ideals in the wake of the collapse of communism, against the poignant backdrop of the Spanish Civil War, a conflict loaded with Irish resonances.

These plays, available for the first time, establish Martin Lynch as a leading Irish playwright of his generation.

Jennifer Johnston
The Desert Lullaby
ISBN: 1 873687 26 5

56 pp, £4.95 pbk

One of Ireland's most import post-war prose writers, Jennifer Johnston has established a reputation as a playwright of rare moral and imaginative force. Her dramatic narratives, *Twinkletoes*, *Mustn't Forget High Noon* and *Christine*—collected by Lagan Press under the title *Three Monologues*—were produced to critical and popular acclaim by the Abbey Theatre, Dublin.

Moving between the Ireland of the 'Emergency' and the present day, *The Desert Lullaby* is the story of two old women: the 'harmless insane' Flora and Nellie, her housekeeper, scold and protector. Their intertwining stories provide an evocative exploration of familial love, oppression, loyalty and memory. Rooted firmly in the imaginative and political tensions at the heart of Ireland past and present, their voices, stories and perspectives—young and old—are an articulation of endurance in the face of greater impersonal forces of destruction: loss, death, decay and betrayal.

By turns comic and harrowing, *The Desert Lullaby* confirms Jennifer Johnston as one of Ireland's most significant dramatists.

Jennifer Johnston's prose works include *The Captain's and the Kings* (1972), *How Many Miles to Babylon* (1974), *Shadows on Our Skin* (1977), *The Christmas Tree* (1981), *The Railway Station Man* (1984), *Fool's Sanctuary* (1987) and *The Invisible Worm* (1991). Her most recent novel is *The Illusionist* (1995).

Sam Thompson
Over the Bridge & Other Plays
edited and introduced by John Keyes
ISBN: 1 873687 66 4
256 pp, £5.95 pbk

"During the Westminster election of 1964, when Lord O'Neill of the Maine was still plain Captain at the Northern Irish helm, he made reference to 'a certain Mr. Sam Thompson whose past experience is, I gather, in producing works of fiction'. A lot of blood has since flowed under the bridge: it is a sarcasm to which posterity has not been kind. Bridges are a favourite Ulster metaphor. 'Bridge building between the communities' has become the compulsory sport of our captains and our kings. The traditional sport of stirring up sectarian hatreds, however, continues to be played at times of stress, like election campaigns, or when deciding upon a suitably provocative name for an actual steel and concrete bridge. Going over the Bridge is another activity entirely, demanding a degree of guts and an integrity which public life in Ireland has failed to cultivate, to say the least. Sam Thompson dedicated his life to it. He coaxed, commanded, persuaded and implored his mulish fellow-countrymen to make the journey. He wasn't a captain or a king but a shipyard painter and they listened to him. They knew the reality of his fiction ... "   —Stewart Parker

Pivotal in the development of modern Irish drama, Sam Thompson marks the début of an authentic urban voice on stage. *Over the Bridge* (1960), produced in the face of hostility from the unionist establishment, is an indictment of sectarianism in people's working lives. His second play, *The Evangelist* (1963), directed by Hilton Edwards to critical acclaim, explores the fanaticism and hypocrisy deforming religion while his last play, *Cemented with Love* (1965) exposes the corruption of political life in the north of Ireland.

Complete with an introduction by critic and theatre historian John Keyes, *Over the Bridge & Other Plays* is a compelling imaginative investigation of the tensions underpinning northern Irish life.